UTOPIA

Utopia

Thomas More

Translated into Modern English
by G. C. Richards
Fellow of Oriel College
Oxford

"The working part of the population of England
carries a mass of non-workers on its back all the
while. . . . We cannot exactly afford so many idle
hands; nor can we afford the numbers of empty
minds England has today."

Stephen Graham

1828 Press

1828
Press

A Baker & Taylor Business
2810 Coliseum Centre Drive
Suite 300
Charlotte, NC 28217

ISBN: 978-1-970184-30-3

Typeset by: Flipside Digital Content Company
Cover design: Samantha A. Meyer
Printed at: Baker & Taylor Publishing Services, Ashland, Ohio

S·M·D
FILIAE CARISSIMAE
PATER

Contents

*Thomae Mori ingenio quid unquam finxit natura vel mollius
vel dulcius vel felicius? Erasmus.*
3 Dec., 1499.

TRANSLATOR'S INTRODUCTION

Thomas More, eldest son of John More, judge in the Court of
Common Pleas (1518) and of the King's Bench (1520), was
born February 7th, 1478, or 1477 as Mr. Nichols more probably holds, in Milk Street, London. He received his early
education at the school attached to St. Anthony's Hospital in
Threadneedle Street, but was removed from school, at a date
which cannot be precisely fixed, to be placed in the household of Cardinal Morton, who as Archbishop of Canterbury
and Lord Chancellor was the most important person in
England after the Sovereign. In the first book of *Utopia* he
makes Hythlodaye give a most pleasant account of the
Cardinal (p. 10), and says himself, 'You have given me great
pleasure . . . while listening to you I felt not only as if I was at
home in my native country, but as if I had gone back to the
days of my youth, being pleasantly reminded of that Cardinal
in whose household I was brought up as a lad' (p. 26). It has
been held that More's History of Richard III, which he wrote
in 1513, was a translation, or rather a free adaptation, of
Morton's Latin. Morton himself is reported by Roper, More's
son-in-law, to have said of the boy to his guests, 'Those of us
who live to see it will find that this child here waiting at the
table will grow into a marvellous man.' Doubtless it was

Morton's influence which sent him to Oxford, when he was at the most fifteen. At Oxford he spent 'not fully two years,' and so took no degree. Whether he was entered at Canterbury College, which was afterward swallowed up in the great foundation of Wolsey, or at St. Mary Hall, or had a connection with both, cannot be stated with any certainty. It seems probable that he made the acquaintance of Colet, who did not leave for Italy till 1493, that he heard the Greek lectures of Grocyn, who returned from Italy in 1490 and did not finally settle in London till 1499, and from his mention of Linacre in his 'Epistle to Dorpius,' that he heard his lectures on Aristotle. Anyhow, this brief academic life must have begun the study of Greek. It was cut short by the determination of his father to allow him no more time for these studies, and to insist on his devoting himself to the law. So he was entered at New Inn, 1494, removed to Lincoln's Inn, 1496, and finally called to the Bar at the age of about 22 or 23 in 1500. In 1499 he made the acquaintance of the great scholar Erasmus, who had been brought to England by his patron, the young Lord Mountjoy. He was profoundly impressed by the learning and wit of the great humanist, who wrote a most life-like description of him to Ulrich von Hutten, 23 July 1519, when all the scholars of the Continent were talking about the English author, whom the *Utopia* had recently made famous. It must have been in the autumn of 1499, when Erasmus was staying at Lord Mountjoy's house at Greenwich, that More and a legal friend played a trick upon him, by taking him a walk to Eltham and introducing him by surprise to the royal children then under the poet Skelton as tutor. Prince Henry, afterward King, challenged the foreign scholar to write something for him, like the verses which More had just offered. Erasmus went home somewhat displeased, and in the course of three days hammered out some verses, though as he says there had been a long divorce between him and the Muses. Soon after this time ('adhuc paene adolescens' says Erasmus) More delivered public lectures in Grocyn's church of St. Lawrence Jewry, on St. Augustine's *De Civitate Dei*, which were largely attended by clergy and men much senior to himself. In 1504 he was returned to Parliament, and there is little doubt, though the details are uncertain, that he signalized himself by opposition to the exorbitant demands of the King, of whom he gives, while not naming him, such an unfavorable picture in *Utopia*, Book I (pp. 32, 33).[1] At this period he became ascetic in his habits, perhaps when he was in enforced retirement from public life, and had thoughts of becoming a Carthusian. But about this time Colet became Dean of St. Paul's and used his influence, as his spiritual director, in the opposite direction. So in June 1505, he married happily, and settled in Bucklersbury, where Erasmus twice visited him, the second time on his return from Italy in 1509, when while waiting for his books he wrote out the *Encomium Moriae*, the material for which he had put together on his journey. His young wife was alive in May 1511, but must have died during the summer; and as Erasmus puts it, 'a few months after her death he married a widow, rather to look after his family than to give himself pleasure, neither very handsome nor young, as he jokingly says, but a vigorous and vigilant housekeeper, and yet with her he lives as amiably and pleasantly as if she were ever so lovely a girl.' Ammonius, the King's Latin secretary, later in the year tells Erasmus that he has moved from More's house to other

---

[1] Germain Brie in his *Antimorus* charges More with censuring Henry VII. in his eulogy of Henry VIII. More can only reply (Allen, 1087) that the evils corrected by the son were due to the father's ill health and bad counselors.

quarters, where he is no better off, but at least does not see 'the hooked beak of the harpy,' an ungallant description of the second Mrs. More. Already in the previous year More had been made under-Sheriff of London (Vice-comes, as the office is called on the title page of *Utopia*), an office of great responsibility and honor, in which he won popularity by his endeavors to settle cases by agreement and his unwillingness to exact fees.

He had paid short visits to Louvain and Paris in 1508, but his first lengthy absence from England was in the spring of 1515, when the London merchants petitioned that he should be made an extra member of the embassy to Flanders, to settle commercial difficulties with the regency of the young Charles, already by right of his mother King of Castile. This embassy kept him away from England for nearly seven months, and was very irksome and expensive to him, but it gave him the great advantage of becoming intimate with Cuthbert Tunstall, an ecclesiastic much versed in diplomacy and no mean scholar (as his letters to Budé, the 'doyen' of French learning, show), whose opinion Erasmus himself quoted to Aldus along with those of Grocyn, Linacre and Latimer, in order to induce the great printer to publish his translation of *Euripides*. It also introduced him to Jerome Busleiden, of Mechlin, whose library and collections of antiques delighted him, and who paid the English author the compliment of writing a commendatory letter for his book. But above all he valued the opportunity of meeting Peter Gilles, the friend and host of Erasmus, who plays so prominent a part in *Utopia*, 'a man so learned, witty and modest, that I would gladly pay a good part of my fortune to be his constant companion': and certainly it is a charmingly ingenuous and frank countenance which Quintin Matsys shows us in the diptych of Erasmus and Gilles, which he painted in

May 1517, for presentation to More. Peter was not very well at the time, and Erasmus, at the advice of a doctor, took some pills, with such bad results that the painter refused to go on with the sittings until he had recovered his proper expression. A good part of More's leisure time, when the duties of the embassy were not pressing, must have been devoted to the composition of Book II of *Utopia*.

Returning to England at the end of the year, he then wrote Book I. The following extracts from Mr. Allen's *Erasmi Epistolae* will fully illustrate the publication of the first edition of *Utopia*. On 3rd September 1516, More writes to Erasmus, 'My *Nowhere* (Nusquama), nowhere well written, I send you with a prefatory letter to my dear Peter. From experience I know there is no need for me to urge you to look after the rest of the business.' Probably about 20th September he writes: 'Some time ago I sent you *Nowhere*, as to which I am anxious it should come out soon, well provided with high recommendations, and if possible not only from scholars but also well-known public men;[2] chiefly because of one person's attitude (I think you will guess who, without my mentioning his name) who, moved by I know not what (you can guess as to that), is sorry that it is brought out before the Horatian nine years.[3] Please look after all this as you think best for me. I should like to know if you have shown, or at least (as I expect you have) described it, to Tunstall. I

[2] More's wish was fulfilled. The book was commended to the public by Jerome Busleiden, a scholarly statesman, and by John Paludanus, Public Orator at Louvain, Gerhard Geldenhauer, Cornelis Schryver and Peter Gilles. The second edition was introduced by Budé, and the third by Erasmus.

[3] Michel's and Ziegler's view, that this is Henry VIII or Wolsey, is ridiculous. Mr. Allen suggests Colet. It might have been Linacre.

should prefer the latter, for then it will be twice pleasing to him, because it will appear more polished through your report than my writing, and because you will relieve him of the trouble of reading it.' On 2nd October Erasmus writes to More from Antwerp: 'As to the Island and the rest, all care shall be taken. . . . Peter Gilles is devoted to you and very much approves of your *Nowhere.*' Erasmus writes to Gilles from Brussels 17th October: 'I am getting *Nowhere* ready. You must send a preface, but not addressed to me but someone else, preferably Busleiden.'

We may suspect that Erasmus, though willing to take all possible trouble in connection with the printing, was a little dubious about the subject matter, and inclined to be critical of the Latinity. In his letter to Hutten he speaks of the first book as written more hurriedly than the second, and so the work, he says, was uneven in style. He often says what a great scholar More would have been if he had been trained in Italy. More's Latinity is certainly, as he himself admits (Allen 424, 116), not as polished as that of Erasmus, but its vigor is unmistakable, and there is so much pathos and 'saeva indignatio' in it, that it often becomes really eloquent. It may be too that Erasmus was not much enamored of communism: the wonder is that Budá swallows it whole, as agreeable to Christ's institution. When Erasmus contributes a prefatory letter to Froben's edition, writing on 25th August 1517 (that is, after the book had already been well received), he says: 'I have hitherto been always pleased beyond measure with all the writings of my friend More, but felt some distrust of my judgment because of the close friendship existing between us. But now that I see learned men unanimously adopting my opinion and even more warmly admiring his remarkable genius, not that they have greater affection but greater discernment, I feel convinced I am right and shall not hesitate in future to express openly what I think.' More writes to Erasmus on 31st October 1516: 'I am delighted that my dear Peter likes my *Nowhere*; if it finds favour with such good judges, it will begin to find favour with me. I shall be glad to know whether Tunstall likes it, or Busleiden or your Chancellor. I scarcely dare to hope for the approval of men so fortunate as to be in the foremost positions in their countries, unless it is gained by the fact that if such great scholars and eminent men lived in my commonwealth, they would certainly be the leading men; while as it is, in their own, however highly they are valued (and of course they are valued highly), they have great rascals equal, if not superior, to them in influence and authority. I do not believe that it will weigh with them, that in such a state they would not have many subjects and inferiors, as kings now describe their peoples, or rather as lower than slaves; for it is far more honourable to govern free men, and such good men have no vestige of that jealousy which wishes others to be badly off, while one is well off oneself.' On 9th November, Busleiden forwards his prefatory letter to Erasmus with a short accompanying note (p. 149). On 12th November, Gerhard Geldenhauer, who corrected proofs for Diericz Martens's press at Louvain, writes to Erasmus: 'Our friend Diericz has gladly undertaken to print *Utopia*. Paludanus will show you a woodcut of the island made by a first-rate artist; if you wish any alteration in it, write or add a note to the drawing.'

On 18th November Erasmus writes to Gilles from Brussels that *Utopia* is in the printer's hands. On 4th December More writes to Erasmus from London to say that he has received a letter from Tunstall complimenting him on his work. 'You cannot think how elated I am, how I have grown in stature and hold my head higher; so constantly do I imagine myself in the part of sovereign of Utopia; in fact I fancy

I am walking with the crown of corn-ears upon my head, wearing a Franciscan cloak, and carrying the corn-sheaf as a sceptre, attended by a great throng of the people of Amaurote. Then would meet us a great procession of ambassadors and foreign potentates, pitiable in comparison of us, showing a foolish pride in coming decked out like children and adorned with women's ornaments, and with chains of that contemptible gold, ridiculous in purple and jewels and such "air-blown trifles."[4] But I should not like you or Tunstall to judge me according to the dispositions of others, who are changed by changing fortunes. Though it has seemed good to Heaven to raise my lowliness to such high estate, as I consider far superior to any monarchy, yet you will never find me forgetful of the old intimacy which I enjoyed with you while yet in the position of a subject. If you do not object to making the small journey and coming to visit me in Utopia, I will see that all who are under my mild sway, shall pay you that honour which is due to those whom they understand to be very dear to their ruler. I should have continued this delightful dream, but alas! the coming of daylight has dispelled the dream and shaken me off my throne and sends me back to the daily mill of the courts. My only comfort is that real reigns do not last much longer.' This extract illustrates well the sportive fancy of the author, to which he gives free rein in addressing his intimate friends. On 15th December he writes to Erasmus 'I am daily expecting my *Utopia*, with the feelings of a mother awaiting the return of a son from abroad.' The book had already come out on 4th January 1517, when Lord Mountjoy writes to Erasmus from Tournay: 'I have received your letter, together with the book about the island of Utopia, with great pleasure, the letter as

[4] Persius *Satires.* V. 19.

coming from a close friend, and the book as the work of one whom, not only for his learning but his close friendship, we value most highly. Owing to the pressure of business I have not yet read the little work, but shall soon peruse it, so that, though I cannot enjoy More's actual society, I can see him in his work.' On 13th January, More writes to Erasmus to say he has written to thank Busleiden for his prefatory letter, and asks him to thank Paludanus and Gilles, who had done their parts to please Erasmus. Clava writes to Erasmus from Ghent on 6th February to say he has ordered and is hourly expecting Thomas More's witty book, and Erasmus replies on 14th February: 'When you read More's *Utopia* you will fancy yourself transported into another world; everything there is so new.' On 18th February, Guy Morillon writing to Erasmus has obviously read the book, for he derives a joke from it.

Mr. Lupton (Introd. p. lxiv) has carefully described the first edition (A). Gilles did his work very badly; for it is full of gross errors. But the 'egregius pictor' did his work well; his initials appear to have been O. N., as these letters are on the flag which waves from the mast of the ship. On 21st February Erasmus writes to Budé at Paris, and recommends him to buy and read *Utopia*, which he will not regret, and similarly on 24th February recommends it to the physician William Cop, as not only amusing, but a shrewd exposition of the sources of the evils which affect almost all governments. Already Erasmus was planning a new edition. On 8th March he asks More to send a corrected copy, and on 30th May (probably) he says he has sent the Epigrams and *Utopia* to Basle to be printed by Froben. On 24th August he writes to Froben's corrector: 'I should like *Utopia* and More's Epigrams to be introduced by a preface from Beatus Rhenanus, and if you approve, they can be united in one volume' (as they were). But there was delay at Froben's press, and meanwhile

Lupset, who was in Paris, apparently at the suggestion of Budé, who now contributed a prefatory letter, procured a new edition (B) near the end of 1517 by the printer Gilles de Gourmont.[5] Erasmus complains of its misprints (5th March 1518); but unjustly, for it corrected a great many misprints of the first edition.

Froben's edition, including Budé's letter to Lupset, which according to Erasmus was made the excuse for the delay, did not appear till March 1518 (C). The woodcut was redrawn and made more artistic, but quite unintelligible; and three figures were added, Hythlodaye being named; his companion is probably intended for More, the third figure cannot be certainly identified. These additions and the title page are ascribed to Ambrose Holbein; the woodcut on p. 13 is signed by Hans Holbein. All the prefatory matter is included with the exception of More's second letter to Gilles (from the 2nd edition) and the letter and verses of Paludanus, which are therefore not translated in this volume.[6] In the edition of November (D) Hans Holbein's drawings alone are retained, and many errors are corrected.

In the *Utopia* we see the fruits of More's experience and reading. On the embassy he contrasted the Flemish towns with his own London, and thus Amaurote, as it once was,

---

[5] Mr. Lupton says, 'What More himself thought of Lupset's proceeding, in getting this printed in Paris, we have no evidence to show.' The fact that this edition contains a fresh letter not included in the first, in which More writing to Gilles keeps up the mystification and vouches for the existence of Hythlodaye, goes far to show that he did not disapprove of Lupset's action. He must have been gratified by the patronage of Budé, a scholar only second to Erasmus.

[6] Budé's epistle to Lupset has been so beautifully rendered by Mr. Lupton, that it seemed impossible to improve on his version.

(p. 51) is to the rebuilt Amaurote, as London to Bruges or Antwerp. The arguments of Hythlodaye against becoming a courtier are just those which More was vainly urging in his own case; for soon after the publication of *Utopia* he was, as Erasmus puts it, dragged to court by Henry VIII. 'No one ever more vigorously sued to be admitted to a court than he endeavoured to avoid it.' But to resist both Wolsey and the King would have been only possible had More been less worth having. 'In that you have been dragged to court, you are lost to us and to letters,' says Erasmus sadly in April 1518. There is much playful wit in *Utopia*, but there is far more bitter satire. No one can read without emotion his description of the eviction of the tenant by the landlord's enclosures, or the manufacture of thieves in preference to the prevention of crime. Ill fed, ill housed, ill clad, the poor man lives a life of grinding toil for an unreasonable number of hours (p. 56).

Many may have equaled, but none has surpassed More in his deep sympathy for the miseries of the many and his indignation at the tyranny of the few, their 'oligopolium' as he terms it. Though he represents himself as combating Hythlodaye's communism and carefully guards himself from time to time against being supposed to agree with the practices described, there can be no doubt that (in spite of his disclaimer, p. 87) he is really expressing his own view when he says that 'Christ instituted all things common' (Budé assents to this too), and when he adds 'that this way of living is still in use among the truest societies of Christians,' meaning monasteries, we cannot doubt that he is in earnest. A very sincere, and even ascetic Christian himself, he is scandalized by the abuses in the Church of his day, bellicose Popes and Bishops (while the Utopian priests prevented slaughter and composed belligerents), preachers who adapt the law of

Christ like a leaden rule to human sinfulness, abbots turning their lands into sheep walks, the excessive number of the clergy lowering the standard of clerical life, and excluding the possibility of real vocation. But we must not suppose that he seriously puts forward cremation or the marriage of priests, or the priesthood of women, or divorce for incompatibility of temper, or the legalization of suicide in case of hopeless disease; and that not merely because he wrote later against some of these things, but because he is writing in the vein of Platonic irony throughout. Where he seems to condemn fasting, he is very careful to guard himself (p. 87).

With equal boldness he lashes the failings of kings—their delight in war rather than in the 'honorable activities of peace,' their faithlessness to treaties, their debasing of the coinage, their obtaining of subsidies on false pretenses, their revival of obsolete laws, and either fining for their non-observance or selling exemption from their provisions, their interference with servile judges, their shameless intrigues against one another. All these things Henry VII did, and most of these Henry VIII did at a later date. The statement that 'the people choose the king for their own sake, and not for his' (p. 45) must have sounded very obnoxious in Tudor ears. 'We wonder,' says Professor Jowett, 'how in the reign of Henry VIII, though veiled in another language, and published in a foreign country, such speculations could have been endured.' It is significant that actually there is no King in Utopia. It is true that More is a little inconsistent with himself. In the facetious letter already quoted, he fancies himself King of the island, and 'Ademus' (p. 59) can hardly be meant to be the title of each of the fifty-four city-mayors: but as a rule, when the 'prince' is mentioned, it means the life-president or mayor of one city-state. For of course the Utopian cities are essentially Greek 'poleis.'

Nor can he have pleased the nobility of the time. He would deprive them of their sports; hunting is 'the meanest part of the butcher's craft.' Their gambling and vulgar pleasures he abhors. Their idle retainers are a menace to society. Their extravagance in pulling down houses and building others on fresh sites ruins themselves and does no one any good. The glory of war and chivalry which they delight in is unreal, and as if to take away all its glamour, he causes the Utopians to use every kind of stratagem and assassination so as to avert or minimize the bloodshed of wars. Their love of gorgeous clothes and jewelry is ridiculed in the description of the Anemolian embassy, which King Henry VIII must almost have thought a reflection on himself.

Who, then, read and appreciated the *Utopia*? The 'Intelligenzia,' not of course those scholastically trained, chiefly ecclesiastics, whose logical methods he ridicules (p. 77), but the humanists in every country, to whom the letters of Erasmus introduce us one by one, who were eagerly studying Greek literature and teaching it. For the *Utopia* is based on the following writings. (i) St. Augustine's *De Civitate Dei*, on which More had lectured to crowded audiences, represented an ideal city, on the lines of which the earthly city might be improved. There is an unmistakable reference to this treatise in II. ix., p. 106, where he speaks of the idea that disasters following a change of religion were due to the anger of the offended deity. His treatment of slavery as penal and corrective in substitution for capital punishment, which Hythlodaye argues against altogether, and which Utopia only admits for certain offenses, is thought by Mr. Lupton to be derived from St. Augustine, (ii) To Plato his debt is much greater. 'In his youth,' says Erasmus, 'he wrote a dialogue to defend Plato's communism, even to the extent of defending community of wives.' This feature is absent from Utopia, where the family is very like that which gathered under More's own roof at Chelsea—grandfather, father and mother, married sons and daughters with their children. The family tie is only broken in Utopia by adoption for the public good, and to enable a man to learn a new trade. But otherwise Plato's writings are the very basis of the *Utopia*. The island Atlantis of the *Critias* suggested the island Utopia as a reformed island of Britain. The kingship of the philosopher is the very basis of Utopian polity: while on the other hand wise men retire from politics as they are (*Rep.* VI. 496). As the guardians of Plato 'must not touch or handle silver and gold, or be under the same roof with them, or wear them, or drink from them,' so it is in Utopia. As women go to battle in the Republic (V. 457) so they do in Utopia. Horses are only kept for youths to develop their riding powers as a military exercise in Utopia (*Rep.* V. 467). He refers to the story in Diogenes Laertius, that Plato refused to draw up a constitution for the Arcadians because they would not have equality of goods. But in one respect he has departed from the *Republic*. There are not three classes in Utopia, but really only one; for all may qualify themselves for the learned class out of which are chosen the magistrates, priests and ambassadors, and the only aristocracy in Utopia is that of intellect. (iii) He seems to have drawn on Cicero's *De Finibus* for his account of the Epicurean and Stoic elements in the Utopian philosophy, though even here he is largely indebted to *Republic*, Book IX. (iv) In several details he seems to have been thinking of Tacitus's *Germania*. In that monograph the Roman historian, though he did not disguise the less admirable side of the Germans, was contrasting their simple life with the degenerate Rome of his day: and so More, while he describes the conduct of the Utopians toward foreign nations as not altogether admirable in war, regards their polity as a great improvement on that of Europe. Their contempt for precious metals is a mark of the Germans, who, moreover, have few laws, whose women go to war, and who make their own clothes; while as the German 'principes' decide on minor matters, but refer weightier ones to the tribal gathering, and never make any important decision on the same day the question is broached, so it is in Utopia.

(v) Many references to Plutarch's *Lives, Laconian Institutions,* and *On Instinct in Animals* have been gathered by editors and show More's knowledge of Plutarch's works. He would owe to Plutarch his knowledge of the common messes of Sparta. (vi) The setting of the dialogue he takes from the *Quattuor Americi Vesputii Navigationes* published in 1507. Hythlodaye is one of the twenty-four left behind by Vespucci at Cape Frio on his fourth voyage, and Utopia is somewhere between Brazil and India. It is also quite possible that More may have met at Antwerp some Portuguese or other mariner who gave him some account of Japan. It was somewhat later that the Portuguese and the Jesuits got a footing in that country, but some knowledge of it may well have reached Europe, while it was known to be closed to foreigners, as was Utopia to all intents and purposes. There is a striking similarity between Utopia's position as regards a continent and that of the islands of Japan, which similarly lie off the mainland in a crescent shape, and at the Strait of Tsushima are divided by a comparatively narrow channel from it, and must have been originally connected with it. The Utopians are (II. vi., p. 88) 'nimble and stronger than would appear from their stature, which is not, however, dwarfish.' In More's day, Japan must have presented to the eye of any intelligent observer the appearance of a well-settled and ordered government, and any traveler's account must have dwelt on the great antiquity of the civilizations of China and Japan (p. 42). Of course More took his communism from Plato and Plato alone.

It remains to describe the Utopian form of government, which is complicated. As there are few laws and no lawyers—More must have had a mean opinion of his brethren in his own profession—a good deal in Utopia depends on prudent administration. Utopia is a federation of fifty-four independent 'poleis,' all of which have the same representative system. In each there is a popularly elected prince or mayor, who holds office for life, if he is not deposed on suspicion of aiming at a tyranny. He is President of a Council of twenty chief officers, who have sitting with them two representatives of the two hundred lower officers changing daily. The Council acts as a High Court of Justice and deals with ordinary matters, but as a probouleutic body refers important matters to the two hundred lower officers, who consult the thirty families of which each is the head. How they collect their views is not stated. The Boule, so to speak, of each town thus consists of twenty-three, the Ecclesia of 200, each of whom represents, or is supposed to represent, the opinion of about, as far as one can judge, 300 adults.

All offices are annual, but the Prince is elected for life. His powers would be similar to those of the Swiss Federal President: his only special function mentioned is that of pardon. To the Federal Council at Amaurote come every year three representatives of each city. This body of 162 members we may assume to have a permanent President, who may have been also Mayor of Amaurote. It has very important functions: (*a*) matters referred from the various cities, (*b*) the supply of commodities to cities that lack them from the surplus of others, (*c*) the fixing of the quantity of goods to be exported, (*d*) the regulation of the population, filling up deficiencies here from excess there, and in case of need, the sending out of colonies, (*e*) the reception of embassies, (*f*) the declaration of war, and the making of peace. The small numbers strike one. Obviously More thought that the educated class, which would be capable of administration, would always be limited in number. But no one could call Utopia an oligarchy: for any masterful person would not be reelected. The citizens so governed live a life which More considers happy; compelled (with few exceptions), it is true, to labor six hours a day, but with intervals for recreation and rest. There is no compulsion to attend the early morning lectures, but they are nevertheless well attended. The benefits of music and cultivation of the mind are open to all; relieved of the crushing load of anxiety for their future livelihood and the support of their families, and removed from all tainting influences from without, they are contented, and there is no possibility of a revolution. Are we wrong in thinking this an ideal which should be aimed at today?

There is, of course, some coercion in Utopia, but Gilles (or possibly Erasmus) thought that its leading note was freedom, as compared with existing conditions; for he comments on the permission accorded to the citizens of having their meals at home if they like, 'as everywhere regard is had to freedom, that nothing should be done by the coercion of the unwilling.'

It may be asked whether anything in the Utopian scheme is possible. It certainly depends on (*a*) isolation, which nowadays is impossible; (*b*) on the close contact of town and country, and the interchange from time to time of agricultural and other workers. Such a system might at any time be tried as an experiment on a small scale. The terrible failure of a communistic scheme in Russia has been due in the first instance to a complete cleavage between town and country, so that it has done nothing but reduce the town dwellers to misery, without in the least helping the countryfolk. (*c*) Compulsory physical training, which is at least highly desirable, is also a necessary condition.

In the following respects More was at least four centuries in advance of his time: in the more favorable position given to women (pp. 66, 96), in the education of women (pp. 57, 74), in the provision of municipal hospitals, in sanitary reform, in the limitation of capital punishment,[7] in the provision for old age, and in the reduction in the hours of labor. If his system could not be applied as a whole to our industrial age—and its author certainly only intended to make men think, and did not put it forward in its entirety as a scheme of reform[8]—it is, nevertheless, a wonderful and epoch-making book.

It is little short of a miracle that the best treatise on the ills of a commonwealth, with the most suggestive thoughts as to the way of avoiding them, should have appeared in the days when absolutism was tightening its hold; and even in these days, when absolutism is everywhere for the moment dead or moribund, we may still turn to the *Utopia*, and not only see, as Professor Brewer has said, the truest picture of the real condition of Europe at that period, but the most truly Christian program ever put forward for the amelioration of human society by the diffusion of culture and the equalization of opportunity to all.

---

[7] The death penalty (apart from war) is mentioned for repeated adultery, for refractory convicts, for offenders surrendered by foreign governments.

[8] Witness his facetious Greek names. The King of 'Nowhere,' is 'he who has no people'; his capital is the shadowy town' on the river 'Waterless.' Their neighbors are the 'Countryless,' the 'Cloud-dwellers,' the 'Blind-Citizens,' and the 'Blessed,' and the narrator is Raphael 'Skilled in Nonsense.' His second letter plainly shows that he meant those acquainted with Greek to see through his fiction, while he desired to keep it up for everyone else.

BOOK I

INTRODUCTORY DISCOURSE OF RAPHAEL HYTHLODAYE ON THE BEST STATE OF A COMMONWEALTH

It chanced that the most invincible King of England, Henry VIII, whose princely virtues are beyond compare, had recently many weighty matters in dispute with His Serene Highness Charles, King of Castile; wherefore to debate of these and reach a settlement he sent me as ambassador to Flanders along with the peerless Cuthbert Tunstall,[1] whom recently, to the great satisfaction of all, he has appointed Master of the Rolls. Of his praises I shall say nothing, not that I fear lest the testimony of a friend may be discredited, but because his merit and his learning are too great for me to describe and too well known to fame for me to attempt the task, unless I should choose to display the brightness of the sun with a candle, as the proverb hath it.

[1] Tunstall was appointed Ambassador to the Court of Brussels in May 1515, and became Master of the Rolls in May 1516. The first edition of the *Utopia* was published at the end of 1516. The second book was written during the course of the embassy, the first after More's return to England at the end of 1515.

We were met at Bruges (this was the meeting place agreed upon) by the commissioners of the King, all notable men, the head of whom was the Margrave of Bruges, but the chief speaker, and the ablest of them all, was George de Theimsecke, Provost of Cassel, a man not only trained in eloquence but a natural orator, moreover most learned in the law, and a clever diplomatist of great experience.[2] When after several meetings there were certain points on which we could not agree, they bade farewell to us for some days, and left for Brussels to learn the will of their King. Meanwhile I, as my business led me, made my way to Antwerp.

While I stayed there, among other visitors to me but most welcome of all, was Peter Gilles, a native of Antwerp, an honorable man of high position in his native place, and worthy of the very highest position,[3] young, and equally distinguished by learning and good character; for he is most virtuous and cultured, to all most courteous, but to his friends so openhearted, affectionate, loyal and sincere, that very few can be found to compare with him as the perfect friend. His modesty is uncommon, no one is less given to deceit, and none has a wiser simplicity of nature. In conversation he is so polished and so witty without offense, that his delightful society and charming discourse took away my home sickness and made me less conscious than before of the separation from my home, wife and children, to whom I was exceedingly anxious to get back; for I had then been more than four months away. One day I had been at divine service in Notre Dame, the finest Church in the city and most crowded with worshippers, and mass being over, was about to return to my lodging,

[2] Cp. Erasmus to More, 3rd June 1516 (Allen 412, I 52).

[3] Gilles was twenty-nine years of age, and held the position of Town Clerk of Antwerp.

when I happened to see him in conversation with a stranger, a man of advanced years, with sunburned countenance and long beard, whose cloak hung carelessly from his shoulder, while his appearance and dress seemed to me to be those of a seafaring man. When Peter espied me, he came up and greeted me, and before I could return his salutation, drew me a little aside and said, pointing to the man I had seen him talking with, 'Do you see this man? I was on the point of taking him straight to you.' 'He would have been very welcome,' said I, 'for your sake.' 'No,' said he, 'if you knew him, for his own. There is no man alive today who can give you such an account of unknown peoples and lands, a subject about which I know you are always most greedy to hear.' 'Well, then,' said I, 'my guess was not a bad one. The moment I saw him, I was sure he was a ship's captain.' 'But you are quite mistaken,' said he, 'for his sailing has not been like that of Palinurus, but that of Ulysses, or rather of Plato.[4] Now this Raphael Hythlodaye, that is his name, is no bad Latin scholar; and most learned in Greek, for he has studied that language more than Latin, because he had devoted himself to philosophy, and in that subject he found that there is nothing valuable in Latin except parts of Seneca and Cicero. So he left his estate at home—he is a Portuguese—to his brothers, and being eager to see the world, joined Amerigo Vespucci,[5] and was his constant companion in the three last of those four voyages, which are

[4] Palinurus was the pilot of Aeneas, the type of the actual mariner. Ulysses was like Hythlodaye in being carried to places he knew nothing of, but Plato's voyages to various Mediterranean countries are given as a better parallel, as Hythlodaye was a deliberate not an unwilling explorer. Hythlodaye seems to be derived from the Greek for 'skilled in idle talk.'
[5] Vespucci's voyages were between 1497 and 1504. His account was first printed in 1507.

now universally read; but in the end he did not accompany him home, for he prevailed on Amerigo to let him be one of the twenty-four who in the last voyage were left behind in the fort.[6] And so, that he might have his way, he was left behind, being more anxious for travel than about the place of his death; for these two sayings are constantly on his lips: " He who hath no grave is covered by the sky,"[7] and "From all places, it is the same distance to heaven."[8] But this determination of his, but for the favor of God, would have cost him dear. However, when after the departure of Vespucci he had traveled through many countries with five companions from the fort, by strange chance he was carried to Ceylon, whence he reached Calicut; and there by good fortune he found some Portuguese ships, and so at length arrived home again, beyond all expectation.'

When Peter had told me this, I thanked him for his kindness in thinking of me and wishing me to have a talk with one whose conversation he hoped would give me pleasure; then I turned to Raphael, and when we had greeted each other and exchanged the civilities which commonly pass at the first meeting of strangers, we went off to my house, and there sat down to talk in the garden on a bench covered with turves of grass.[9]

He told us how, after the departure of Vespucci, he and his friends who had stayed behind in the fort, began by

[6] At Cape Frio in Brazil.

[7] Lucan VII. 819. 'Caelo tegitur qui non habet urnam.'

[8] Cic *Tusc* I. § 104, 'undique ad inferos tantundem viae est.'

[9] In the Basle edition, 1518, a woodcut is introduced with the scene in the garden. The seat seems to be a framework of wood enclosing earth and grass. To the left is John Clement, then follow Hythlodaye, More (treated as in the picture of the island) and Gilles.

degrees through continued meetings and civilities to ingra-
tiate themselves with the natives, till they not only stood in
no danger from them, but were actually on friendly terms,
and moreover were in favor and good repute with a chief
(whose name and country I have forgotten): by his generosity ample provision and journey money were supplied for
himself and his five companions, and, moreover, a trusty
guide on their journey (which was partly by water and partly
in carriages over land) to take them to other Princes with
careful recommendations to their favor. For after traveling
many days, he said, they found towns and cities and very
populous commonwealths with excellent institutions. To be
sure under the Equator and on both sides of the line, as far
as the sun's orbit extends, there lie waste deserts, scorched
with continual heat. A gloomy and dismal region extends on
all sides, without cultivation or clearing, inhabited by wild
beasts or men no less savage and harmful than are the beasts.
But when you have gone a little farther, gradually the country assumes a milder aspect, the climate is less fierce, the
ground covered with a pleasant green herbage, and the living creatures less wild. At length you reach peoples, cities
and towns, which maintain a continual traffic by sea and
land, not only with each other and their neighbors, but also
with far-off countries. Then they had opportunity of visit-
ing many countries in all directions, for every ship which
was got ready for any voyage made him and his companions welcome as passengers. The ships they saw in the parts
they first came to were flat-bottomed, and the sails were
made of papyrus stitched together on withies, and sometimes made of leather. Afterward they found ships with
pointed keels and canvas sails, in fact in all respects like our
own, and mariners skilled in adapting themselves to sea and
weather. But he reported that he won their favor by showing

them the use of the magnetic needle, of which they had hitherto been quite ignorant, so that they had hesitated to trust themselves to the sea, and only did so in the summer; but now, trusting to the loadstone, they did not fear stormy weather, being dangerously confident. Thus there is a risk that what was thought likely to be a great benefit to them may, through their inexperience, cause them great mischief. What he said he saw in each place, it would be a long story to tell, and is not the purpose of this work. Perhaps on another occasion I shall tell his story, particularly what would be useful to readers, such as those good and wise institutions, which he noticed in nations living in civil order and polity. For on these subjects we eagerly inquired of him, and he no less readily discoursed. But about the conventional travellers' wonders we were not curious. For Scyllas and greedy Harpies and cannibal Laestrygonians are common enough, but well and wisely trained citizens are not everywhere to be found. But just as he called attention to many ill-advised customs among these strange nations, so he rehearsed not a few points, from which our cities, nations, races, and kingdoms may take example for the correction of their errors, which, as I said, I must mention on another occasion. Now I intend merely to relate what he told us of the manners and customs of the Utopians, first, however, giving the discourse which led him on to mention that commonwealth.

For when Raphael had touched with much wisdom on faults of both parts of the world, of which he found very many in both, and had compared the wise measures that have been taken both here and there—for he remembered the manners and customs of each nation as if he had lived all his life in places which he had only visited—Peter expressed his surprise as follows: 'Why, Master Raphael, I wonder that you do not attach yourself to the court of some king. I am sure there is none of them to whom you would not be very welcome, because you are capable not only of entertaining a king with this learning and experience of countries and people, but also of furnishing him with examples and assisting him with counsel. Thus you would not only serve your own interests excellently but be of great assistance in the advancement of all your relations and friends.' 'As for my relations and friends,' quoth he, 'I am not greatly troubled about them; for I think I have fairly well performed my duty to them already. For the possessions (which other men do not resign unless they are sick and old, and even then resign unwillingly) I divided among my relations and friends when I was not merely hale and hearty, but actually young, and I think they ought to be satisfied with this generosity from me and not to require or expect that I should, for their sakes, enter into servitude to kings.' 'Softly, my good Sir,' said Peter, 'I meant not that you should be in servitude but in service to kings.' 'The one is only one syllable less than the other,' said he. 'But my opinion is,' said Peter, 'whatever name you give to this mode of life, that it is the very way by which you can not only profit both individuals and the commonwealth, but also render your own condition more prosperous.' 'Should I,' said Raphael, 'make it more prosperous by a way which my soul abhors? As it is, I live as I please, which I fancy is very seldom the case with your grand courtiers. Nay, there are plenty of those who court the friendship of the great; and so you need not think it a great loss if they have to do without me or a few like myself.' 'Well,' said I, 'it is plain that you, Master Raphael, are desirous neither of riches nor power, and assuredly I reverence and look up to a man of your mind, no whit less than to any of those who are most high and mighty. But, methinks, you will do what is worthy of this generous and truly philosophic spirit of yours, if you so order your life as to apply your talent and industry to the public interest, even if it involves some disadvantage to yourself. This you can never do with as great profit as if you are counsellor to some great prince, and make him follow, as I am sure you will, straightforward and honorable courses. For from the prince, as from a never-failing spring, flows a stream of all that is good or evil over the whole nation. But you possess such complete learning that even had you no great experience of affairs, and so great experience of affairs that even had you no learning, you would make an excellent member of any king's council.' 'You are twice mistaken,' said he, 'first in me, and then in the matter in question. For I have no such ability as you ascribe to me, and if I had ever so much, yet by disturbing my own peace and quiet, I should not promote the public interest. For in the first place, almost all princes prefer to occupy themselves in the pursuits of war (with which I neither have nor desire any acquaintance) rather than in the honorable activities of peace, and care much more how, by hook or by crook, they may win fresh kingdoms, than to administer well what they have got. Besides among the counsellors of kings there is none who is not really so wise that he does not need to profit by the counsel of another, or who does not think himself so wise that he does not wish to profit by it, save that they agree with the most absurd sayings and play the parasite to those whose favor they desire to win by flattery, because they are chief favorites with the king. And to be sure, it is but human nature that each man favors his own inventions most, just as the crow and the monkey like their own offspring best. But if anyone in that company, where some are jealous of others' inventions or prefer their own, should propose something which he has either read of as done in former times or has seen done in other places, they behave as if their whole reputation for wisdom were endangered, and as if afterward they would deserve to be thought blockheads, if they could not lay hold of something to find fault with in the inventions of others. If all else fails, they take refuge in this as a last resort. "These things," they say, "were good enough for our ancestors, and we only wish we were as wise as they were." With this, which they regard as an unanswerable argument and a conclusion of the whole matter, they resume their seats. As if indeed it were a dangerous thing for anyone to be found wiser than his ancestors, whose wise provisions we are content to leave alone; but if he suggests that in any matter wiser measures might have been taken, that gives us a handle for censures of him which we never let go. Such proud, ridiculous and obstinate prejudices I have encountered in other places, and once in England.' 'What,' said I, 'were you ever in our country?' 'Yes,' said he, 'I once spent several months there, not long after the disastrous end of the Cornish rising[10] against their king, which was put down with such bloodshed. During that time I was much indebted to the Right Reverend Father, Cardinal John Morton, Archbishop of Canterbury, and at that time also Lord Chancellor of England, a man, Master Peter, (for Master More knows about him, and needs no information from me) who deserved respect as much as for his wisdom and virtue as for his authority. He was of middle stature and showed no sign of his advanced age; his countenance inspired respect rather than fear; in intercourse he was agreeable, though serious and dignified. By rough address he sometimes made trial of those who made suit to him, but in a harmless way, to see what ability in answering and presence of mind a man

[10] The Cornish insurgents were defeated at Blackheath on June 22nd, 1497, two thousand being killed.

possessed, which virtue, provided it did not amount to impudence, gave him pleasure as akin to his own disposition, and excited his admiration as suited to those holding public office. His speech was polished and to the point. His knowledge was profound, his ability incomparable, and his memory wonderfully retentive: for by learning and practice he improved his natural qualities. The King placed much confidence in his advice, and when I was there, the state seemed to depend upon him. For in early youth he had been taken straight from school to court, had spent his whole life in important public affairs, and had had many vicissitudes of fortune, so that by many and great dangers he had acquired his sagacity, which, when thus learned, is not easily forgotten. It happened, one day, that I was at his table, when a layman, learned in the laws of your country, was present, and in the course of conversation began to speak highly of the strict justice which was then dealt out to thieves, who were everywhere executed, as many as twenty at a time being hung on one gallows, and added that he wondered all the more, though so few escaped execution, by what bad luck the country was infested with them. I was free to express my opinions without reserve at the Cardinal's table, so I said to him, "You need not wonder; for this manner of punishing thieves goes beyond justice and is not for the public good. It is too harsh a penalty for theft and yet is not a sufficient deterrent. For theft alone is not an offense that ought to be punished with death; and no penalty that can be devised is sufficient to restrain from brigandage those who have no other means of getting a livelihood. And so, in this respect not your country alone, but the greater part of the world resembles bad schoolmasters, who would rather beat than teach their scholars. For you ordain grievous and terrible punishments for theft, when it would have been much better

to provide some means of getting a living, that no one should
be under this terrible necessity, first of stealing and then of
dying for it." "We have," said he, "made sufficient provision
for this; there are handicrafts and there is agriculture; they
might maintain themselves by these, if they did not prefer to
be rascals." "No," said I, "you shall not escape so easily. We
will say nothing of those who often come home maimed
from foreign or civil wars, as recently with you from the
fight with the Cornishmen and not long ago from the war in
France,[11] men who lose their limbs in the service of state or
king, and whose infirmity prevents them from exercising
their old crafts, and age from learning a new one. Of these, I
say, we will take no account, for wars come intermittently
and are not continuous; but let us consider what happens
every day. Now there is a great number of noblemen, who
not only live idle themselves like drones on the labors of others, as for instance the tenants of their estates, whom they
squeeze to the utmost by raising their rents (for that is the
only economy they know of, being otherwise so extravagant
as to bring themselves to want), but also carry about with
them a huge crowd of idle followers, who have never learnt a
trade for a livelihood. These, as soon as their master dies, or
they themselves fall sick, are turned out at once; for the idle
are maintained more readily than the sick, and moreover,
the heir is not always able to maintain as large a number of

[11] Henry VII cannot have lost many men in his French war. In 1487 he
promised to assist his former protector Francis, Duke of Brittany,
against Charles VIII, but did not keep his word. In 1489 he sent an
army to protect Anne, but with instructions not to fight. After Anne
had accepted the hand of Charles, an English army did lay siege to
Boulogne in October 1492, but by the Treaty of Etaples, November 14,
Henry accepted an indemnity and retired.

serving men as his father did, at any rate at first. So in the meantime their energies are devoted to starving, if they be not to thieving. Indeed what can they do? For when by a vagabond life they have worn out their clothes and their health to boot, sickly and ragged as they are, no gentleman will engage them, and the country folk dare not do so either, knowing full well that one who has been softly brought up in idleness and luxury and has been wont to ruffle it in sword and buckler, looking down with a swaggering face on the whole neighborhood, and thinking himself far above everybody, will not be fit to render honest service to a poor man with spade and hoe, for scanty wage, and on frugal fare." "But this," replied he, "is just the sort of men we ought to encourage and make much of; for on them, as being men of a more lofty and manly spirit than artisans and husbandmen, depend the strength and sinews of our army when we have to wage war." "To be sure," said I, "you might as well say that for the sake of war we must foster thieves. For while you have these men, you will certainly never be without thieves. Nay, as robbers are no bad soldiers, so soldiers are not the most cowardly robbers: so well do these two pursuits agree. But this defect, though frequent with you, is not peculiar to you; for it is common to almost all peoples. France in particular is troubled with another more grievous plague. Even in peace time (if you can call it peace) the whole country is crowded and beset with mercenaries, for they are like you, convinced that it is a good thing to keep these idle retainers. For these wiseacres[12] think that the safety of the commonwealth depends on having always in readiness a strong and reliable garrison, chiefly of veterans; for they have no confidence in

---

[12] Morosophi 'foolishly wise,' a word found in Lucian. Sully called James I. 'the wisest fool in Christendom.'

untrained men. And therefore they have always to be seeking for a pretext for war, that they may not have men without experience and ignorant how to cut throats, lest, to use Sallust's witty saying, 'the hand or the mind through lack of practice become dulled.'[13] Yet how dangerous it is to rear such wild beasts, France has learned to its cost, and the examples of Rome, Carthage, Syria, and other nations show; for not only their empires, but their land, and even their cities have been more than once destroyed by their own standing armies. Now, how unnecessary it is to maintain them is clearly proved by this: not even the French soldiers trained in arms from infancy can boast that they have very often got the better of your conscripts; not to say more, for fear of seeming to flatter you to your faces.[14]

"'Nor are your town-bred artisans, or your rough and untrained husbandmen supposed to be much afraid of the idle followers of gentlemen, except those whose build of body is unfitted for strength and bravery, or whose spirit is broken by poverty. So there is no danger that those, whose bodies, once strong and vigorous (for it is only the picked men that gentlemen deign to corrupt), are now either weakened by idleness or enfeebled by occupations fit only for women, should be made effeminate, if trained to earn their living by honest pursuits and practiced in manly toil. But, however this may be, it seems to me by no means profitable to the common weal, to keep a vast multitude of such people,

---

[13] Sallust Catiline, c. 16.

[14] Erasmus (Allen 360) writing 2nd October 1515, after the battle of Marignano, in which Francis defeated the Swiss, says: 'Our friends the Swiss are very angry with the French for not politely giving way before them in battle, as they did before the English.' He refers to the flight of the French at the battle of the Spurs, 16th August 1513.

as trouble and disturb peace, for the emergency of a war, which you never have unless you choose it; and yet you ought to think far more of peace than of war.[15] But this is not the only thing that makes thieving necessary; but there is another, which, as I believe, is peculiar to you alone." "What is that?" said the Cardinal. "Your sheep," said I, "which are usually so tame and so cheaply fed, are now, it is said, so greedy and wild, that they devour men, and lay waste and depopulate fields, houses and towns. For in those parts of the realm where the finest and therefore most costly wool is produced, these nobles and gentlemen, and even holy Abbots, not satisfied with the revenues and annual profits derived from their estates, and not content with leading an idle life and doing no good to the country, but rather doing it harm, leave no ground to be tilled, but enclose every bit of

[15] Cp. Johnson—*A Journey to the Western Islands.* 'It must be confessed that a man who places honour only in successful violence is a very troublesome and pernicious animal in times of peace; and that the martial character cannot prevail in a whole people but by the diminution of all other virtues. He that is accustomed to resolve all right into conquest, will have very little tenderness or equity.'

Machiavelli. *The Prince,* ch. XII

'That prince who founds the duration of his government upon his mercenary forces will never be firm or secure; for they are divided, ambitious, undisciplined, unfaithful, insolent to their friends, abject to their enemies, without fear of God or faith to men; in time of peace they divorce you, in time of war they desert you, and the reason is because it is not love nor any principle of honour that keeps them in the field; it is only their pay, and that is not a consideration strong enough to prevail with them to die for you; whilst you have no service to employ them in, they are excellent soldiers; but tell them of an engagement, and they will either disband before or run away in the battle.'

land for pasture, pull down houses, and destroy towns, leaving only the church to pen the sheep in.[16] And, as if enough English land were not wasted on parks and preserves of game, these holy men turn all human habitations and cultivated land into a wilderness. Thus in order that one insatiable glutton and plague of his native land may join field to field and surround many thousand acres with one ring fence, many tenants are ejected and, either through fraud or violence, are deprived of their goods, or else wearied by oppression are driven to sell. Thus by hook or by crook the poor wretches are compelled to leave their homes—men, women, husbands, wives, orphans, widows, parents with little children and a family not rich but numerous, for farm work requires many hands: away they must go, I say, from their familiar and accustomed homes, and find no shelter to go to. All their household furniture, which would not fetch a great price if it could wait for a purchaser, as it must be thrust out, they sell for a trifle; and soon, when they have spent that in moving from place to place, what remains for them but to steal, and be hung, justly forsooth, or wander about and beg? And yet even then they are put in prison as vagrants, for going about idle, when, though they eagerly offer their labor, there is no one to hire them. For there is no farm work, to which they have been bred, to be had, when there is no plough land left. For one shepherd or herdsman is sufficient for eating up with stock land for whose cultivation many hands were once required, that it might raise crops. And so it is that the price of food has risen in many parts. Nay, the

[16] 'Great men makithe nowadays
   A sheepecott in the Churche.'
Furnivall, *Ballads from MSS.,* I. 97. cp. Brewer, *Reign of King Henry VIII* vol. I. (Petition to the Parliament of 1514.)

price of wool has grown so high that the poor, who used to make cloth in England, cannot buy it, and so are driven from work to idleness. For after the great increase in pastureland, a plague carried off a vast number of sheep, as though God were punishing greed by sending a murrain upon the sheep, which should more justly have fallen on the owners' heads. But, however much the number of sheep increases, the price does not fall, because if you cannot call that a monopoly which is not a sale by one person, it is certainly a sale by few persons; for all has come into the hands of a few rich men, who are not obliged to sell before they wish, and do not wish until they get the price they ask. By this time all other kinds of stock are high priced, both for the same reason, and, still more so, because as the farmhouses have been pulled down and the tillage is lessened, there are none left to devote themselves to the breeding of stock. For these rich men will not rear the young beasts as they do lambs; but they buy them lean and cheap abroad, and then when they are fattened in their pastures, sell them again at a high price. And so, as I suppose, the whole mischief of this system has not yet been felt. For so far these methods only raise the prices, where the animals are sold; but when for some time they have been removing them from other parts faster than they can be bred there, then as the supply gradually diminishes in the markets where they are purchased, there must needs be great scarcity here. Thus the unscrupulous greed of a few is ruining the very thing by virtue of which your island was once counted fortunate in the highest degree.[17] For the high price of food is

---

[17] Robinson interprets More as meaning the hospitality and open house kept by the great in England. Perhaps More is only thinking of the support and maintenance given to a large number by noblemen, and the lamentable condition of a retainer when dismissed.

causing everyone to get rid of as many of his servants as possible, and what, pray, have they to do but to beg, or become robbers, which is a course more natural to men of high spirit? Moreover, alongside of this wretched need and poverty you find wanton riotousness of living. For not only the servants of noblemen but artisans and almost the rustics themselves, in fact all classes alike, are given to much ostentatious sumptuousness of dress and excessive indulgence of the table. Do not brothels, stews, wineshops, alehouses, and all those games of chance, cards, dicing, tennis, bowls, and quoits, soon drain the purses of their votaries and send them off to rob others, when their money is gone? Cast out these ruinous plagues; make laws that those who have destroyed farmhouses and country towns should either restore them or hand them over to those who will do so, and are ready to build. Restrict this right of rich people to buy up everything and keep a kind of monopoly for themselves. Let fewer be brought up in idleness. Let agriculture be restored. Let cloth working be introduced once more, that there may be honest occupation to employ usefully this idle crowd, those whom hitherto poverty has made thieves, or who are now vagabonds or lazy servants, and in either case likely to become thieves. Assuredly unless you remedy these evils, it is useless for you to boast of the justice you execute in the punishment of theft, which is more showy than really just or beneficial. For when you allow your youths to be very badly brought up and even from early years to become more and more vicious, to be punished of course, when as grown-up men they commit the offenses, which from their boyhood they had shown every prospect of committing, what do you do but first create thieves and then punish them?"

'Even while I was speaking, the lawyer had been preparing himself to reply, and had determined to adopt the usual method of disputants, who are more careful in repeating what has been said, than in answering it, so highly do they regard the memory. "Certainly, Sir," said he, "you have spoken well, considering that you are but a stranger, and have been able to hear something of these matters rather than to get exact knowledge of them, which I will briefly make clear. For first I will repeat in order what you have said; then I will show in what respects ignorance of our conditions has deceived you; finally I will demolish and destroy all your arguments. So to begin with what I promised first, in four respects you seemed to me—" Here the Cardinal interrupted him and said, "Hold your peace, for it looks as if your reply would be lengthy, if you begin thus. So we will relieve you of the trouble of making your answer now, but you shall reserve your right unimpaired till your next meeting, which provided neither you nor Master Raphael are hindered by other business, I should like to fix for tomorrow. But now I should like you to tell me, Raphael, why you think that theft ought not to be punished with death, and what other penalty you would fix, which would be more beneficial to the public; for I am sure you do not think it ought to go unpunished. But when even as it is, with death as the penalty, men still rush into stealing, what force and what fear, if they once were sure of their lives, could deter the criminals, who would regard themselves as much invited to crime by the mitigation of the penalty as if a reward were offered?" "Certainly," said I, "right reverend father and my kind lord, I think it quite unjust that a man should lose his life for the loss of money. For in my opinion not all the goods that fortune can bestow on us can be set in the scale against a man's life. But if they say that this penalty is attached to the offense against justice and the breaking of the laws, and not to the theft of money, one may well style this extreme justice as extreme wrong.[18] For we ought not to approve of such stern rules[19] of law as should justify the drawing of the sword, when they are disobeyed in trifles, nor on the other hand such Stoical[20] ordinances as count all offenses equal, so that there is no difference whether one kills a man or robs him of a coin, when if equity has any meaning, there is no similarity or connection between the two cases. God has said, 'Thou shalt not kill,' and shall we so lightly kill a man for taking a little money? But if the divine command be held not to apply where the law of man justifies killing, what prevents men equally from arranging with one another how far adultery, fornication and perjury are admissible? For God forbids a man not only to take the life of another but also his own; but if when men by mutual consent have agreed on definite cases where human life may be taken, their will ought to prevail so far as to exempt from the bonds of His law such of their followers who, without any example set by God, yet take the life of those whom human ordinance has commanded to be put to death, will not thus the law of God be valid only so far as the laws of man permit? And the result will be that in the same way men determine in everything how far it suits them, that the commandments of God should be obeyed. Finally the law of Moses, though severe and harsh, being intended for slaves, and those a stubborn people, nevertheless punished theft by fine and not by death. Let us not suppose that God in the new law of mercy, in which He gives commands as a father to his sons, has allowed

---

[18] This is the Latin maxim 'summum jus summa injuria.'

[19] Manlius condemned his son to death for disobedience (Livy VIII. 7. 22); hence 'Manliana imperia' became proverbial for stern decrees.

[20] The later Stoics held that all crimes were equal. Cicero *Pro Murena* 29; Horace *Sat.* I. 3. 96.

us greater license to be cruel to one another. These are the reasons why I think this punishment unlawful. Now how absurd and even dangerous to the commonwealth it is that a thief and a murderer should receive the same punishment, surely everyone knows. For since the robber sees that he is in as great danger if merely condemned for theft as if he were convicted of murder as well, this consideration alone impels him to murder a man, whom otherwise he would only have robbed; for besides the fact that he is in no more danger if caught, there is greater safety in putting the man out of the way, and a greater hope of covering up the offense, if there is no one left to tell the tale. And so while we try to frighten thieves with excessive cruelty, we urge them on to the destruction of honest men.

"'Now, as to the question that is often put, what punishment can be more suitable; in my judgment it is much easier to find than what can be worse. For why should we doubt that that is a good way of punishing crime, which we know was practiced of old by the Romans, the greatest experts in government, and found favor with them so long? When men were convicted of great crimes they condemned them for life to stone quarries and to dig in mines, to be kept constantly in chains. Yet, as concerns this, I can find no better custom in any nation than that which in the course of my travels I noticed in Persia among the people commonly called the Polylerites,[21] a large and well-governed nation, and except that they pay an annual tribute to the Persian king, in all other respects free and autonomous. They are far from the sea, and almost ringed round by mountains; and being satisfied with the products of their own bounteous

---

[21] An imaginary name from the Greek πολὺς λῆρος 'much nonsense'; a people whose existence it would be nonsense to suppose.

land, neither visit others often nor receive visits, and in accordance with their ancient custom, they do not try to enlarge their territory; and what they have is easily protected from all aggression by the mountains, and the tribute they pay to their overlord. Thus they are completely free from military service, and live a life more comfortable than conspicuous, and happy rather than renowned or famous; for even their name is hardly known except to their immediate neighbors. Now in their land those who are convicted of theft, repay to the owner what they have taken from him, not, as is usual elsewhere, to the King, who they think has as little right to the thing stolen as the thief. But if the thing is lost, the value is made up and paid out of the goods of the thieves, the residue being reserved intact to their wives and children, and they themselves are condemned to hard labor; and unless the theft was outrageous, they are neither confined in prison nor wear fetters, but without any bonds are set to public works. If they refuse to work or are slack, they are not put in chains but urged on by the lash. If they do a good day's work, they need fear no taunt or reproach. Every night their names are called over and they are locked in their sleeping quarters. Beside the constant toil their life has no hardship. For as servants to the commonwealth, they are fed well at the public expense, the mode varying in different places. In some parts what is spent on them is raised by almsgiving; and though this method is precarious, the people are so kindhearted that it is found to supply the need most plentifully. Elsewhere public revenues are set aside to defray the cost. In some places all pay a fixed tax for these purposes. In some parts the offenders do no work for the community, but when a private man needs a hired laborer, he hires in the market place the labor of one of them for a day at a fixed wage, somewhat lower than what he would have paid to a free man. Moreover it is permitted to chastise any of these serving men with stripes, if he be idle. So they are never out of work; and beside their food each of them brings something into the public treasury every day. One and all are dressed in clothes of the same color.

"'Their hair is not shaved, but cropped a little above the ears, from one of which the tip is cut off. Food and drink and clothes of the proper color may be given them by their friends, but it is a capital offense that money should be given them, both for the giver and the receiver; and it is no less dangerous for a free man to receive money for any reason from one so condemned; or for slaves, which is the name the convicts bear, to touch weapons. The slaves of each district are distinguished by a special mark, which it is a capital offense to throw away; as it is to be seen beyond their own bounds, or to talk to a slave from another district. And it is no less risk to plan escape than actually to run away. Nay, the punishment for connivance in such a plan is death for the slave, and slavery for the free man. On the other hand rewards are appointed for one who gives information—for a free man money, and for a slave, his freedom, and to both pardon and impunity for their complicity, that it never may be safer to follow out an evil purpose, than to repent of it. This is the law and order of the matter, as I have described it to you. You can easily see how humane and advantageous it is. The object of this anger is to destroy vices and save the persons, their treatment being such as of necessity to make them good, and by the rest of their lives to repair the damage they have done before. So little is it to be feared that they may sink back into their old evil ways, that even travelers who have to go a journey think themselves most safe, if they obtain as guides these slaves, who are changed from time to time as they come to a fresh district. For they have nothing suitable about them with which to commit robbery; their hands are unarmed, money would merely ensure the detection of the crime; if caught, punishment awaits them and there is absolutely no hope of escape. For how could a man so direct his flight as to escape observation, when he resembles other men in no part of his attire, unless indeed he were to run away naked, and even then his ear would betray him? But it may be said that there is risk of their taking counsel together and conspiring against the state; as if any neighborhood could conceive such an idea without having first sounded and seduced the slaves of many other districts, who are so little able to conspire together that they may not even meet and converse or greet one another. Much less will they boldly divulge the plot to their companions, when they know that it is dangerous if concealed, but very profitable if betrayed. But, on the other hand, no one is quite without hope of the possibility of some day recovering his liberty by obedience and patience, and by showing a good prospect of living a reformed life in future; for no year passes in which some are not restored to freedom, being recommended by their patient endurance."

'When I had said this and added that I saw no reason why this method might not be adopted in England too, and be more beneficial in its working than the justice which my opponent had praised so highly, the lawyer said, "Nay, this could never he established in England without bringing the state into the greatest danger," and so saying he shook his head and made a wry face, and so held his peace. And all who were present, gave him their assent. Then the Cardinal said, "It is not easy to guess whether it would turn out well or ill, inasmuch as the experiment has not been made. But if after sentence of death had been pronounced, the King were to postpone its execution, and were to try this method, first limiting the privileges of sanctuary,[22] then if the event proved its utility, it would be right that it should be law; in the other case, to put to death those who were previously condemned would be no less for the public good and no more unjust than if it were done now; and in the meantime no danger can come of the experiment. Moreover, I am sure that vagabonds might quite well be treated in the same way; for in spite of repeated legislation, we have not made much progress in dealing with them." When the Cardinal had said this, they all vied in praising what they had received with contempt when suggested by me, but especially the part relating to vagabonds, because it was the Cardinal's addition.

'What followed then, perhaps it were better to suppress; for it was very absurd, but I will relate it; for it was not bad in itself and had some bearing on the matter. There was present a parasite, who seemed to want to imitate a jester, but he was too near the truth in his sayings to be in jest: his ill-timed witticisms were meant to raise a laugh, but he himself was more often the object of laughter than his jests. However, sometimes the fellow let fall observations which were to the point, thus proving the proverb true, that if a man throws the dice often he will sooner or later make a lucky throw. So when one of the guests said that, as by my proposal a good provision had been made for thieves, and the Cardinal had also taken precautions for vagabonds, it only remained now that public provision should be made for those whom sickness or old age had brought to want and made unable to work for their living. "Give me leave," said the man, "I will see that this, too, is set right. For I am very anxious to get this sort of person out of my sight; so often have they harassed me with their pitiful

[22] More deals with the abuse of the right of sanctuary in his *History of Edward V.*

whinings in begging for money, though they never could pitch a tune which would get a coin out of my pocket. For one of two things always happens: either I do not want to give, or I cannot, since I have nothing to give. So now they have begun to be wise, for when they see me pass by, they say nothing, and spare their pains, expecting nothing from me, any more than if I were a priest. But I would have a law passed that all beggars should be distributed and divided among the Benedictine monasteries, and the men be made lay brethren, as they call them, and the women nuns." The Cardinal smiled and allowed it in jest; but the others in earnest. Now a certain friar, who was learned in theology, was so delighted by this jest at the expense of priests and monks, that he, too, began to make merry, though generally he was serious even to sourness. "Nay," said he, "not even so will you be rid of beggars, unless you make provision for us friars too." "Well, but this has been done already," said the parasite. "For his Eminence made excellent provision for you, when he determined that vagabonds should be kept in order and made to work; for you are the greatest vagabonds of all." When the company saw, by looking at the Cardinal, that he did not take this jest amiss any more than the other, they all began to approve of it except the friar, for he—and I do not wonder—stung by this taunt,[23] began to be so furious and enraged, that he could not refrain from abuse; he called the man a rascal, railer, whisperer, and son of perdition, quoting the while terrible denunciations out of Holy Scripture. Now the scoffer began to scoff in earnest and was quite in his element. "Don't be angry," said he, "good friar; for it is written 'In your patience ye shall possess your souls.'" Then the Friar replied—I will

---

[23] More uses the phrase of Horace, *Satires* I. 7. 32: 'drenched with such vinegar.'

repeat his very words—"I am not angry, rogue; or at least I do not sin; for the Psalmist says, 'Be ye angry, and sin not.'" Then the Cardinal gently admonished the friar to calm his feelings, but he replied, "Nay, my lord, I speak not but of good zeal, for holy men had good zeal, wherefore it is said, 'The zeal of thy house hath consumed me,' and we sing in Church—'The scorners of Elisha, while he went up to the house of God, felt the zeal of the bald head,' as perchance this ribald scoffer shall feel it." "Perhaps," said the Cardinal, "you do it of a good affection, but I think you would behave, if not more holily at any rate more wisely, if you did not set your wits against those of a silly fellow, and provoke a foolish contest with a fool." "Nay, my lord," said he, "I should not do more wisely; for the wise Solomon said, 'Answer a fool according to his folly,' as I do now, and show him the pit into which he will fall, if he take not good heed. For if many scoffers of Elisha, who was only one bald head, felt the zeal of the bald, how much more will one scorner of many friars, among whom many are bald? Moreover, we have a Papal bull by which all who scoff at us are excommunicate." When the Cardinal saw there was no making an end, by a motion of his head he dismissed the parasite, and turned the conversation to another suitable subject, and soon afterwards rose from table and dismissed us, going to hear the petitions of his suitors.

'There, Master More, with how tedious a tale I have burdened you; I should have been quite ashamed to do so if you had not eagerly called for it, and seemed to listen as if you did not want any part of the conversation to be left out. This I had to relate, though somewhat cursorily, to exhibit the judgment of those who, though they rejected what I said at the time, yet immediately afterward, when the Cardinal did not disapprove of it, gave their approval too, flattering him so much that they even smiled on and almost allowed in earnest the fancies of the parasite, which his master in jest did not reject. So from this you may judge how little regard courtiers would pay to me and my advice.' 'To be sure, Raphael,' said I, 'you have given me great pleasure; for what you have said has been both wise and witty. Besides, while listening to you I felt not only as if I were at home in my native country, but as if I had gone back to the days of my youth, being pleasantly reminded of the Cardinal in whose household I was brought up as a lad.[24] And since you are so devoted to his memory, you cannot think how much more attached I feel to you on that account, attached as I was to you already. But even now I cannot change my mind, but must needs think that if you could persuade yourself not to shun the courts of kings, you could do the greatest good to the common weal by your advice;[25] and this is the most important part of your duty, as it is the duty of every good man. For since your favorite writer Plato is of opinion that states will only be happy if either philosophers are kings or kings turn to philosophy,[26] what a distant prospect there will be of happiness if philosophers will not even deign to impart their counsel to kings.' 'They are not so ungracious,' said he, 'that they would not gladly do it—indeed many have done it by published books— if the rulers would be ready to take good advice. But doubtless

---

[24] Thomas More was first sent to St. Anthony's school in Threadneedle Street, but was soon removed to the household of Cardinal Morton, where he stayed till his fifteenth year, when he went to Oxford, perhaps in 1492.

[25] Ammonius writing to Erasmus, 18th February 1516, says: 'After honourably discharging his embassy, More has come home from your Netherlands and is as constant an attendant at Court as myself. He is the earliest to pay his morning call on the Cardinal of York.'

[26] *Republic*, Book V. 473.

Plato was right in foreseeing that if kings did not turn to philosophy themselves, they would never approve of the advice of real philosophers, being themselves from their youth infected and saturated with wrong ideas; this he found from his own experience with Dionysius.[27] So if I proposed beneficial measures to some king, and tried to uproot from his mind the seeds of evil and corruption, do you not think that I should be forthwith banished or treated with ridicule? Come now, suppose I were at the court of the French king, and sitting in his Privy Council, while in a gathering of his most astute counsellors under his own presidency, they were all setting their wits to work to consider by what crafty devices he might keep his hold on Milan,[28] and bring back Naples

[27] Dionysius the younger became tyrant of Syracuse in 367 BC. Through the influence of Dion, his brother-in-law, Plato was invited to Syracuse, but his influence was only short lived, and after Dion's banishment, he left Syracuse.

[28] Charles VIII. of France (1483–1498) invaded Italy in 1494 to wrest the Milanese from the Sforza family and to assert the Angevin claim to the throne of Naples, but had no success. Louis XII. (1498–1515) in 1499 occupied the Milanese, and attempted to drive out Frederick the Aragonese king of Naples. The latter appealed for help to Ferdinand, King of Aragon, who sent Gonzalo of Cordova with a Spanish army. At first a partition of Naples was agreed upon by a secret arrangement between Louis and Ferdinand, but in 1503 the French were driven out and Naples was still being governed by Spanish viceroys when More wrote. Louis was driven out of Italy in 1512, but Francis I (1515–1547), on succeeding his cousin, won back the Milanese by the victory of Marignano, 13th Sept. 1515. Francis was taken captive at Pavia in 1525, and by the peace of Cambray, 1529, abandoned the Milanese, Flanders and Artois, when Charles V. abandoned his claim to that part of the Burgundian dominion which is French today. The two French occupations of Milan lasted respectively from October 1499 to May 1512, and from October 1515 to November 1521.

into his power which has for the time eluded his grasp; then subsequently destroy Venice, and subjugate the whole of Italy; then bring under his sway Flanders, Brabant and the whole of Burgundy, and other nations too, over which he has already conceived the idea of becoming King. And suppose that one advises that treaty should be made with the Venetians to last only so long as he shall find it convenient, and that he should make common cause with them, and even deposit in their keeping part of the booty, which, when all has gone according to his mind, he may reclaim; while another recommends the hiring of German lanzknechts, and another the winning of the Swiss by money; another advises propitiating the offended majesty of the Emperor with gold as an acceptable offering;[29] another thinks that a settlement should be made with the King of Aragon, and the independent kingdom of Navarre be ceded to him as a guarantee of peace;[30] another proposes that the King of Castile shall be caught by the prospect of a marriage alliance,[31] and that some nobles of his court shall be drawn over to the King's side by a fixed pension. Meanwhile the most perplexing question of all is, what is to be done with England? But they agree that negotiations for peace should be entered

---

[29] The Emperor Maximilian was notoriously always in want of money. He was accepting money from both France and England, till he deserted the English alliance by the Treaty of Noyon, 1516.

[30] After the death of Isabella, Ferdinand married Germaine de Foix in order to assert his claim to Navarre, and in 1512 succeeded in annexing that part of the kingdom which lay south of the Pyrenees.

[31] On Francis I's accession there were negotiations to arrange a marriage between Charles and Renée, the four-year-old daughter of Louis XII. He finally accepted a betrothal to the infant Anne, the French waiving their claim to Naples. Brewer, *Reign of Henry VIII*. I. 140 and 154.

into, and an alliance always weak should be strengthened with the strongest bonds, so that the English should be called friends but should be suspected as enemies. The Scots therefore must be posted in readiness, ready for any opportunity to be let loose on the English if they make any movement.[32] Moreover, some exiled noble must be secretly fostered[33]— for treaties prevent it being done openly—to maintain a claim to the throne, that by this handle he may keep in check a king in whom he has no confidence.

'In such a case when such efforts were being made and each was vying with the other in proposals of a warlike nature, what if an insignificant person like myself were to get up and advise going on another tack, leaving Italy alone and staying at home, and to argue that the kingdom of France by itself was almost too large to be well governed by a single man, so that the king should not think of adding other dominions to his sway, and if then I put before them the decisions taken by the people called the Achorians, who live on the mainland to the southeast of the Island of Utopia? They had gone to war to win for their king another kingdom, to which he said he was the rightful heir in virtue of an old alliance of marriage. But after they had secured it, they saw they would have no less trouble over keeping it

[32] While Henry VIII was engaged with the Emperor Maximilian in attacking France by way of Flanders and occupied with the siege of Terouenne, his brother-in-law James IV of Scotland declared war, invaded England, and lost his life at Flodden, September 9th, 1513.

[33] 'He had taken the precaution of sending Albany into Scotland with a large sum of money. If this project failed, he had still a card to play in the *White Rose*, Richard de la Pole, the exiled claimant of the Dukedom of Suffolk, whom Francis fostered, pitied and cajoled with promises of restoration to the crown of England.' Brewer, *ib.* I. 97.

than they had suffered in obtaining it, for there were constantly springing up in the country thus acquired the seeds
of rebellion within or of invasion from without, and thus
they would have had to fight constantly for them or against
them, and to keep an army in constant readiness; while in
the meantime they were being plundered, and money was
being taken out of the country, they were losing their lives
for a little glory to others, peace was no more secure than
before, their morals at home were corrupted by war, the
lust for robbery had become universal, recklessness of
human life widespread, and the laws were held in contempt,
because the king being distracted with the charge of two
kingdoms, could not properly attend to either. And so at
length, seeing that in no other way would there be any end
to all this mischief, they took counsel together, and courteously but firmly offered their king his choice of retaining
which of the two kingdoms he preferred; because he could
not keep both, as there were too many of them to be ruled
by half a king, just as no one would care to engage even a
muleteer whom he had to share with someone else. So the
worthy king was obliged to be content with his own realm
and hand over the new one to one of his friends, who was
driven out soon afterward.

'Furthermore, if I proved that all these attempts at
warfare, by which so many nations were kept in a turmoil
on the French king's account, would, after draining his
resources and destroying his people, at length by some mis-
chance be brought to naught, and therefore he had better
look after his ancestral kingdom, and make it as rich and
flourishing as possible, love his subjects, and be loved by
them, live with them and rule them gently and have no
designs upon other kingdoms, since what he had already
was more than enough for him, what reception, friend

More, think you, would this advice of mine find?' 'To be sure, not a very favorable one,' said I. 'Well, then, let us proceed,' said he, 'suppose the counsellors of a king debating with him and devising by what schemes they may heap up treasure for him. One advises the raising of the value of money when he has to pay any, and the lowering of its value below what is right when he has to receive any, that he may discharge a large debt with a small sum, and where only a small sum is due to him, receive much.[34] Another suggests a make-believe war, under pretext of which he would raise money, and then when he thought fit make peace with great solemnity, to throw dust in the eyes of the people, because forsooth the good king had compassion on his people and would fain avoid bloodshed.[35] Another reminds him of old and moth-eaten laws, which no one remembers being made and therefore everyone has transgressed; he should exact fines for their transgression, there being no more rich source of profit, nor any more honorable than such as has an outward appearance of justice.[36] Another recommends him under heavy penalties to prohibit many things and especially such as it is to the people's advantage not to allow, and afterwards for money give a dispensation to those whose interests are interfered with by the prohibition. Thus favor is won with the people, and a double profit is made, both by fines from those whose greed of gain has entangled them in the snare, and by selling privileges to others at a

[34] An allusion to Edward IV and Henry VII's treatment of the coinage.
[35] Henry VII obtained subsidies for a war with France in 1492, and immediately concluded the peace of Étaples.
[36] Empson and Dudley are alluded to, who 'filled the royal coffers and extended the royal authority by the revival of obsolete penal statutes and by an unjust employment of the royal right of escheat' (*Bright*).

higher price; and forsooth the higher the price, the better the prince, who, since he dislikes to give anyone an indulgence which is contrary to the common welfare, will not do so except at a high price. Another persuades him that he must bind to himself judges who will in every case decide in favor of the royal prerogative, and to do this he must summon them to the palace and invite them to debate his affairs in his own presence; so there will be no cause so unjust in which one of them will not, either from a desire to contradict, or from shame at repeating another's view, or to curry favor, find some loophole whereby a false accusation may be set up. Thus when through the opposite opinions of the judges a thing clear as daylight has been made a subject of debate, and truth becomes a matter of doubt, a convenient handle will be given to the king to interpret the law to his own interest, all the rest will acquiesce from shame or fear, and then sentence will boldly be pronounced from the Bench; for a pretext can never be wanting for deciding on the king's side. For it is enough for him that either equity is on his side or the letter of the law, or the wrested meaning of what is written, or what outweighs all law with conscientious judges, the undoubted prerogative of the king's majesty. Thus all the counselors agree and consent to the saying of Crassus,[37] that no amount of gold is enough for a king who has to keep an army: further that a king, however much he wishes, can do nothing wrong; for all that all men possess is his, as are they themselves, and so much is a man's own as the king's generosity doth not take away from him, and that it is much to the king's interest that this should be as little as possible, seeing that his safeguard lies in the fact

[37] Pliny Natural History XXXIII. 10. 'M. Crassus negabat locupletem esse, nisi qui reditu annuo legionem tueri posset.'

that the people do not grow wanton with riches and freedom, because these things make them less patient to endure
harsh and unjust commands; while on the other hand poverty and need discourage them and make them patient,
taking away from the oppressed the generous spirit of
rebellion. Hereupon, suppose again I were to rise and maintain that these counsels were both dishonorable and
dangerous for the king, whose very safety, not merely his
honor, rested on the people's resources rather than his own;
and should show that they choose their king for their own
sake and not for his, that by his labor and effort they may live
well and safe from injustice and wrong; so that it belongs to
the king to take more care for the welfare of his people than
for his own, just as it is the duty of a shepherd *qua* shepherd
to feed his flock rather than himself.[38] And the facts show
that they are quite wrong in thinking that the poverty of the
people is a safeguard of peace. For where will you find more
quarrelling than among beggars? Who is more eager for
revolution than he who is discontented with his state of life?
Who is more reckless in the endeavor to upset everything,
in the hope of getting profit from some source or other,
than he who has nothing to lose? Now if there were any king
who was so despised or hateful to his subjects, that he could
not keep them in subjection otherwise than by ill usage,
plundering and confiscation, it would surely be better for
him to resign his throne than to keep it by these means, by
which, though he retain the name of authority, he loses its
majesty. For it is not consistent with the dignity of a king
to exercise authority over beggars, but he should rule over
rich and prosperous subjects. This was certainly the opinion of that noble and lofty spirit, Fabricius, who said that he

[38] Cp. Plato Republic, Book I. 343.

would rather be a ruler of rich men than be rich himself.[39] To be sure, that one man should live a life of pleasure and self-indulgence amid the groans and lamentations of all around him, is not to be the keeper of a kingdom but rather of a prison. In fine, as he is an incompetent doctor who cannot cure one disease except by creating another, so he who cannot amend the lives of citizens in any other way than by depriving them of the good things of life, must admit that he does not know how to rule free men. He had better amend his own self-indulgence or pride; for it is generally through these vices that the people either despises or hates him. Let him live harmlessly on what is his own, let him adjust his expenses to his revenues, let him check evildoers, and by training his subjects aright, let him prevent rather than allow that to grow up which he will have afterward to punish; let him not be hasty in putting into force laws long fallen into disuse, especially those which have long been given up and never were needed; and let him never take as confiscated property anything that a judge would not suffer a private person to appropriate, because he would be crafty and unjust if he did.

'What if then I were to put before them a law of the Macarians, a people not very far distant from Utopia? Their king, on the day he first enters into office, after solemn sacrifices, is bound by an oath that he will never have at one time in his coffers more than a thousand pounds of gold or its equivalent in silver. They say this law was instituted by a very good king, who cared more for his country's good than his own

[39] Fabricius was the Roman general who refused the bribes of Pyrrhus, King of Epirus, when he invaded Italy. This saying is attributed by Valerius Maximus IV. 5 to his successor, M' Curius Dentatus, who finally defeated Pyrrhus in 275 BC.

wealth, to be a barrier against hoarding so much money as would cause poverty among his people. For he saw that this treasure would suffice the king to put down rebellion or defend the kingdom in case of having to meet a hostile invasion; but that it was not large enough to tempt him to invade the possessions of others. This was the chief cause for which the law was made; and the next was, that he thought provision was thus made against any scarcity of money required for the daily buying and selling of the citizens; and when the king has to pay out anything that comes into his treasury beyond the limit prescribed by law, he thought he would not seek occasion to commit injustice. Such a king will be both a terror to the evil and beloved by the good. If I tried to obtrude these and other such warnings on men strongly inclined to the opposite way of thinking, to what deaf ears should I preach!'

'Deaf indeed, without doubt,' said I, 'and I am not surprised. Nor, to tell the truth, do I think that such topics should be thrust on people, or such advice given, as you are sure will never be listened to. For what good could such novel topics do, or how could they enter the minds of those who are already taken up and possessed by the opposite conviction? In the private intercourse of friends this philosophy of the schools is not without its charm, but in the councils of kings, where great matters are debated with great authority, there is no room for these things.' 'That is just what I meant,' said he, 'by saying there is no room for philosophy with kings.' 'Yes there is,' said I, 'but not for the philosophy of the schools, which thinks that everything is suited to every place; but there is another philosophy, more suited to citizens, which knows its own stage, adapts itself to that, and in the play that is in hand, performs its own part neatly and appropriately. This is what you must employ.

Otherwise, while a comedy of Plautus[40] is being performed and the household slaves are making trivial jokes at each other, if you come on the stage in a philosopher's attire and recite the passage from the "Octavia" where Seneca is arguing with Nero,[41] would it not be better to have taken a part without words, than by reciting something inappropriate to have made a hotchpotch of tragedy and comedy? For you will have spoiled and upset the actual play by bringing in irrelevant matter, even if your contribution is superior. Whatever play is being performed, perform it as well as you can; and do not upset it all, because you bethink you of another which has more wit. So it is in the commonwealth with the deliberations of kings. Suppose wrong opinions cannot be plucked up by the root, and you cannot cure, as you would wish, vices of long standing, yet you must not on that account abandon the ship of state and desert it in a storm, because you cannot control the winds. But neither must you impress upon them new and strange language, which you know will carry no weight with those of opposite conviction, but by indirect approach and covert suggestion you must endeavor and strive to the best of your power to handle all well, and what you cannot turn to good, you must make as little bad as you can. For it is impossible that all should be well, unless all men are good, which I do not expect for a great many years to come.' 'By these means,' said he, 'I should accomplish nothing, but share the madness of others, while I attempted to cure their lunacy. For if

[40] Twenty comedies adapted from Greek originals by Plautus (250–154 BC) are extant.
[41] The 'Octavia' is preserved among the tragedies of Seneca, the philosopher and tutor of Nero, all powerful during the first five years of his reign. The scene alluded to is in the second act.

I would stick to the truth, I must needs speak in the manner I have described; to speak false things may, for all I know, be the part of a philosopher, but it is not for me. Yet though perhaps my language may be unwelcome and disagreeable to them, yet I cannot see why it should seem strange to the extent of folly. But if I told them the kind of things Plato imagines in his *Republic*, or what the Utopians actually put in practice in theirs, though such institutions were superior (as to be sure they are) yet they might seem strange, because here we have the right of private property, while there all things are common. But my discourse, apart from the fact that it would be addressed to those, who had made up their minds to go headlong by the opposite path, could not be agreeable because it would beckon them back and point out dangers ahead; otherwise what did it contain that it would not be appropriate or desirable to have said everywhere? Truly if all things which by the perverse ways of men have come to seem strange are to be dropped, as unusual and absurd, we must suppress almost all the doctrines of Christ, which He forbade us to suppress, so much so that what He had whispered in the ears of His disciples, He commanded to be proclaimed openly upon the housetops. The greater part of His teaching was far more different from the life and manners of mankind than was my discourse. But preachers, crafty men that they are, following I suppose your advice, since they found that men disliked to have their manners fitted to the rule of Christ, adapted His teaching to men's manners, as if it were a rule not of iron but of lead,[42] that at least in some way or other the two might be joined together.

[42] A leaden rule was used in Lesbian building because it could be easily adapted to curved moldings. More has got the expression from Aristotle's *Ethics* V, 10, 7.

By this I cannot see what they have gained, except that men may be bad with fewer qualms of conscience. And certainly I should do as little good in the councils of Kings. For I should either have a different opinion, which would come to the same thing as if I had none, or else the same, when I should, like Mitio in Terence,[43] help and share their madness. For as to the indirect approach and covert suggestion of which you speak, I cannot see what object it has; I mean your advice to use my best endeavors, if all things cannot be made good, that they should at least be handled well, and made, as far as may be, as little bad as possible. For at Court there is no room for dissembling, nor can you shut your eyes to things; you must openly approve of the worst counsels, and subscribe to the most ruinous decrees. He will be counted as a spy and almost as a traitor, who so much as gives scant praise to evil counsels. Moreover, there is no chance for you to do any good, when you are brought into the company of colleagues, who would more easily corrupt the best of men than be themselves reformed; by their evil conversation you will either be seduced yourself, or keeping your own integrity and innocence you will be made a screen for the wickedness and folly of others, far from being able to make anything better by your indirect approach and covert suggestion. This is why, in a fine image Plato[44] shows why, philosophers are right in abstaining from political life. For when they see the people rushing out into the streets and soaked by incessant showers, and cannot induce them to go indoors and escape the rain, while they know that if they

[43] Terence *Adelphi* 1. 2. 66. Verum si augeam Aut etiam adiutor sim eius iracundiae, Insaniam profecto cum illo. We have six plays by Terence (185–159 BC).

[44] *Republic,* Book VI., 496.

go out, they can do no good but will only be wetted with the rest, they keep at home, being content if they are at least safe themselves, since they cannot cure the folly of others. Yet surely, Master More, to tell you what I think myself, it seems to me wherever you have private property, and all men measure all things by money, there it is scarcely possible for a state to have justice or prosperity, unless you think there is justice, where all good things come into the hands of the evil, or prosperity, where all is divided among very few, and even they are not altogether well off, while the rest are downright wretched. Wherefore when I ponder on the wise and holy institutions of the Utopians, among whom, with very few laws, things are ordered so well that virtue has its reward, and yet with equality all men have abundance of all things; and then when I contrast with their manners so many nations ever making fresh laws, and yet never in any case provided with laws enough—states in which whatever a man has got possession of, he calls his own private property, but where all these laws that are daily framed are not enough for a man to secure, defend, or even to distinguish from the goods of others what each in turn calls his own—this is readily shown by the endless and ever rising and interminable lawsuits—when, I say, I consider all this, I become more partial to Plato and wonder less, that he refused to make laws for those who rejected that legislation which gave to all an equal share of all good things.[45] For the wise sage easily foresaw, that it was the one and only road to the welfare of a state, if equality in all respects were enforced, and that this could never be preserved, where private property existed. For when by certain titles every man turns all that he can to

[45] The story is taken from Diogenes Laertius III. 17 (Aelian *Var Hist.* II. 42). It seems to refer to the foundation of Megalopolis, 370 BC.

his own use, be there never so great abundance of wealth, it is all shared by a few, and the rest are in poverty; and it generally happens, that the one class deserves the lot of the other, for the former are greedy, unscrupulous and useless, while the latter are well behaved, simple and by their daily labor more profitable to the commonwealth than to themselves. So sure I am that no just and even distribution of goods can be made, nor any perfect happiness be found among men, unless private property is utterly abolished. While it lasts, there will remain a heavy and intolerable burden of poverty and anxieties for the greatest and best part of mankind. I admit that this can be relieved to some extent, but I maintain it cannot be removed. A statute might be made that no one should hold more than a certain amount of land, and that no one should have an income beyond that permitted by law; laws might be passed providing that no king should be too powerful and no people too overweening, that offices should not be sued for nor bought and sold, and that no one should be put to any expense in holding them—otherwise an opportunity is given them of recouping themselves by fraud and robbery and it would be necessary to appoint rich men to offices which should rather have been held by wise men; by such laws, I say, as sick bodies which are past cure can be kept up by constant medical treatment, so these evils, too, can be alleviated and made less acute; but there is no hope of a cure and a return to healthy conditions, while each man is master of his own property. Nay, while you are engaged with the cure of one part, you make the sores of the other worse; thus the disease of the one arises from the healing of the other, since nothing can be added to one man without being taken away from another.' 'But I am of the contrary opinion,' said I, 'that life can never be happy or satisfactory, where all things are common. For how can there be a sufficient supply of goods, when each withdraws himself from the labor of production? For he has not the motive of personal gain, and he is rendered slothful by trusting to the industry of others. But when they are driven to labor by poverty[46] and yet a man cannot by any law keep as his own what he has gained by his labor, must there not be continual trouble from bloodshed and revolution? especially as the authority of magistrates and respect for their office is removed; for how there can be any place for that among men who are all on the same level, I cannot even conceive.' 'I marvel not,' said he, 'that you think so, for you either have no conception at all or else a false one of the state of things I mean. If you had been with me in Utopia and had personally seen their manners and customs, as I did (for I lived there more than five years, and would never have wished to go away but for the desire of making known that new world), you certainly would admit that you had never seen a well-ordered people anywhere but there.' 'Yet surely,' said Peter Gilles, 'it will be hard for you to convince me, that a better ordered people is to be found in the new world than in that known to us, in which I imagine there are as good wits and older institutions than theirs, and in which long experience has invented very many conveniences for human life, not to speak of the chance discoveries made among us, which no wit could have devised.' 'As for the age of states,' said he, 'you could give a better opinion if you had read the histories of that world; if we may believe them, there were cities there, before there were men here.[47] As to what wit has invented or chance discovered, that might

---

[46] There is no poverty in Utopia. Whether the desire of possession can be eliminated, is a point on which there is much discussion today.

[47] Cp. Introduction.

have happened equally in both places. But I certainly think that, even granting that we surpass them in wits, we are far inferior to them in perseverance and industry. For according to their chronicles, up to our arrival they had never heard anything about us, whom they call the *Ultraequinoctials*, except that 1200 years ago a ship driven by tempests to the island of Utopia was wrecked there. Some Romans and Egyptians were cast on shore, and remained in the island without ever leaving it. Now mark what a good use their industry made of this one opportunity. There was no art which could be turned to any use within the Roman empire, which they did not either learn from the shipwrecked strangers, or find out for themselves after thus receiving the impulse to inquiry; so great an advantage was it to them, that on this one occasion some strangers were carried to their coasts. But if the like fortune has ever carried someone from their country to ours, it is as completely forgotten, as perhaps it will be forgotten in time to come, that I was once there. And though they straightway at the first meeting appropriated to themselves any good invention of ours, yet I suppose it will be long before we receive and adopt anything which is better ordered with them than with us. This, I think, is the chief reason why, though we are inferior to them neither in wit nor in wealth, their commonwealth is more wisely governed and more prosperous than ours.' 'Well, Raphael,' said I, 'I beseech you, give us a description of the island, and do not be brief, but set forth in order, the land, the rivers, the cities, the inhabitants, the manners, customs and laws, in fact everything which you think we should like to know. And you may think we wish to know everything of which we are as yet ignorant.' 'There is nothing,' said he, 'I shall be more pleased to do; for I have the facts ready to hand, but it will take time.' 'Then,' said I, 'let us go in to dinner; and afterward we will take up as much time as we like.' 'Be it so,' said he. So we went in and dined, and after dinner we returned to the same spot, sat down on the same bench, and after giving orders to the servants that we should not be interrupted, Peter Gilles and I urged Raphael to fulfill his promise. So when he saw us intent and eager to listen, after sitting in silent thought for a time, he thus began his tale.

Book II

Chapter One

Of the Island of Utopia

The island of Utopia in the center where it is broadest, extends for two hundred miles, and this breadth continues for the greater part of the island, but toward both ends it begins gradually to taper. These ends form a circuit of about 500 miles, and so make the island resemble the new moon, the horns of which are divided by a strait about eleven miles across, which then opens out into a wide expanse. As the winds are kept off by the land which almost surrounds it, it is like a huge lake, unruffled and not subject to storms, and thus converts almost all the center of the country into a harbor, in which ships can go in every direction to the great convenience of the inhabitants. The mouth of this sea between the horns is rendered dangerous by shallows and rocks. Near the center of the gap stands one great crag, which being visible, is not dangerous. It has a tower built on it which is occupied by a garrison. The other rocks are hidden, and therefore treacherous. The channels are only known to the natives, and so it does not often happen that any foreigner enters the gulf except with a Utopian pilot; for the entrance is hardly safe even for themselves; but they are guided in their course by landmarks on the shore. If these were removed and placed in other positions, they could easily destroy an enemy's fleet, however numerous. On the opposite coast there are numerous harbors, but the landing is everywhere so well defended by nature or by art, that a few defenders can prevent a strong force from effecting a descent. As is reported, and as the appearance of the ground shows, the island was once not surrounded by sea. But King Utopus, whose name as conqueror the island bears, (up to then it was called Abraxa),[1] who brought a rude and rustic nation to such a perfection of civilization and refinement as makes them now superior to almost all other peoples, having gained a victory at his first landing, ordered an extent of fifteen miles on the side where the land was connected with the continent, to be dug up, and caused the sea to flow round the land. Having set to the task not only the inhabitants, but to prevent them from thinking the task imposed upon them a disgrace, his own soldiers also, he thus divided the work among so many hands, that it was finished with incredible quickness; and the neighbors, who at first had derided the undertaking as vain, were struck with wonder and terror at his success.

The island contains 54 cities or county towns, all large and fine, identical in language, manners, customs and laws, similar in situation, and everywhere, where the nature of the ground permits, the same in appearance. None of them is less than twenty-four miles from the next, but none is so isolated that you cannot go from it to another in a day's

[1] Abraxa (1) may be 'unwetted,' cp. the river Anyder (waterless); (2) or from the Gnostic 'Abraxas,' as in ch. 9 'Mithras' is the name given to the chief god.

journey on foot. From each city three old and experienced citizens meet once a year at Amaurote,[2] the capital, to discuss the affairs of common interest to the island; for the city being in the very center of the country is most conveniently situated for the representatives of all parts. The territories are so well assigned to the cities, that each has at least twenty miles of land on every side, and on some sides more, where the towns are farther apart. No town has any desire to extend its territory, for they count themselves the cultivators rather than the owners of what they hold. Everywhere in the country they have, at suitable distances from each other, farmhouses well fitted with the implements of agriculture. They are inhabited by citizens who come in succession to live there. No rural household numbers less than forty men and women, besides two slaves attached to the soil, and over each is set a grave master and mistress of ripe years. Over every thirty households is set a Phylarch.[3] Twenty from each household return every year to the city, having completed two years in the country. In their place the same number are sent fresh from the city, to be instructed by those who have been there a year and are therefore more expert in husbandry, and will themselves teach others in the following year; thus there is no danger of any mistake or want of skill causing scarcity, as might happen, if all at one time were newcomers and without knowledge of farming.

Though this system of changing the cultivators of the soil is the rule, to prevent anyone being forced against his will to continue long in a life of hard work, yet men who take a natural pleasure in agricultural pursuits, obtain leave to stay several years. The occupation of the cultivator is to till the

---

[2] Amaurote, the obscure or 'spectral' city, cp. Homer' ἀμαυρόν.
[3] Phylarch, in Greek, 'the ruler of a tribe.'

ground, to feed the animals, to get wood and to convey it to the town by land or water, as is most convenient. They breed a great quantity of poultry by a wonderful contrivance. For the hens do not sit on the eggs, but by keeping a great number of them in a uniform heat they bring them to life and hatch them. The chickens as soon as they have come out of the shell, follow and know human beings instead of hens. They breed very few horses and these only high-spirited ones, which they use for no other purpose than for exercising their young men in horsemanship. All the labor of cultivation and transport is performed by oxen, which, as they say, are inferior to horses in a sudden spurt, but far superior to them in staying power and endurance, and not liable to so many diseases; moreover it takes less trouble and expense to feed them, and when they are past work they come in usefully for food.

They sow corn only for bread. Their drink is wine, either made of grapes or of apples and pears, or sometimes pure water, often that in which they have boiled honey or licorice, of which they have a great quantity. Though they know for certain, how much corn the city and its adjacent neighborhood requires, they produce far more corn and cattle than they require for their own use and distribute the remainder among their neighbors. Whenever they require anything which is not found in the country, they send for all this stuff from the city, and without having to give anything in exchange, easily obtain it from the city magistrates. For many go there every month on the recurring holiday. When the time of harvest is at hand, the Phylarchs in the country inform the city magistrates, what number of citizens they require to be sent to them; and this number of harvesters, coming at the appointed time, in one day, if it be fine weather, complete almost all the harvest work.

CHAPTER TWO

OF THE CITIES, AND ESPECIALLY OF AMAUROTE

He who knows one of the cities will know them all, so exactly alike are they, except where the nature of the ground prevents. So I will describe one or other; for it does not matter which I choose, but which should I rather than Amaurote?[1] For none is worthier, the rest deferring to it because it is the meeting place of the Council; and none is better known to me, for I lived in it five years without a break.

Amaurote is built on the gentle slope of a hill, and is almost four-square. Its breadth is about two miles starting

[1] Amaurote is like the London of More's time (1) in being on a tidal river some distance from the sea; (2) in having a stone bridge over the river; (3) in its water supply; (4) in having walls on three sides but none along the river; (5) in having gardens, which London had only in the suburbs. It is unlike London (1) in the position of the bridge; (2) in having a dry ditch; (3) streets twenty feet broad; (4) each house having a back entrance into a common garden; (5) three-storied houses in regular rows solidly built, with flat concrete roofs and windows filled with glass or with oiled cloth. The improvements which More wished to see were no doubt suggested to him by his visits to Bruges and Antwerp on his embassy to the Low Countries.

from just below the crest of the hill and running down to the river Anyder; its length by the side of the river is rather more than its breadth. The river rises eighty miles above Amaurote from quite a small spring, but being increased in size by various tributaries, two of which are of fair size, before it reaches the city, it is half a mile broad,[2] and soon becomes still broader. After a further course of sixty miles it falls into the ocean. For through the whole distance between the city and the sea, and even above the city for some miles, the tide flows rapidly in for six hours at a time, and then ebbs with equal speed. When the sea comes in, it fills the whole bed of the Anyder with its water, for a distance of thirty miles, and drives the river back. At such times it turns its water salt for some distance farther; but after that the river becomes gradually sweet and passes the city untainted, and when the ebb comes, the fresh water extends almost down to the mouth of the river. The city is joined to the opposite bank of the river not by a bridge of piles or timber stakes, but by a stone bridge with fine arches, placed at the corner of the city which is farthest from the sea, so that ships may pass along the whole of that side of the city without hindrance. They have also another river, not large, but very gentle and pleasant, which rises out of the same hill on which the town is built and runs down through its middle into the river Anyder. The source of this river just outside the city has been connected with it by outworks, lest in case of a hostile attack the water may be cut off, or rendered unfit for drinking. From this point the water is distributed by brick channels into various parts of the lower town; where the ground makes that impossible, the rainwater collected in big cisterns is just as useful. The town is surrounded by a high

[2] Cp. More's letter to Gilles (five hundred or three hundred paces?).

and broad wall with towers and outworks at intervals. A ditch, dry but deep and broad and made impassable by thorn hedges, surrounds the walls on three sides; on the fourth the river takes the place of the ditch. The streets are well laid out both for traffic and to avoid the winds; the houses, which are in no way mean, are set together in a long continuous row faced by a corresponding one; and these house fronts are divided by a road twenty feet broad. On the back side of the houses, through the whole length of the street, lies a broad garden enclosed on all sides by the backs of the streets.

Every house has not only a door into the street but a back door into the garden. Folding doors, easily opened by hand and closing of themselves, give admission to anyone so that there is no privacy. Every ten years they actually exchange their houses by lot. They are very fond of these gardens; in them they have vines, fruits, herbs, flowers, so well kept and flourishing, that I never saw anything more fruitful or elegant anywhere. Their zeal is increased not merely by the pleasure afforded them, but by the keen competition between streets, which shall have the best-kept garden. Certainly you cannot find anything in the whole city more productive of profit and pleasure to the citizens, and there was nothing which the first founder cared so much for as these gardens. For they say that the whole city was laid out first by Utopus himself, but he left to posterity to add the adornment and general ordering of it, for which he saw one lifetime would not suffice. So it is stated in their chronicles (these are preserved most carefully written out and embracing the history of 1760 years), that at first the houses were low, mere hovels and cabins, with mud walls and ridged roofs thatched. But now all the houses are of handsome appearance with three stories, the surface of the walls being made of flint or plaster or brick, rubble being only used in the interior. The roofs are flat and covered with a kind of cement which is cheap, but so well mixed that it is impervious to fire, and superior to lead in defying the violence of storms. They keep the winds out of their windows by glass, which is in very common use, or sometimes by thin cloth smeared with oil or amber. This has two advantages: more light is let in, and the winds are better kept out.

CHAPTER THREE

OF THE MAGISTRATES

Every thirty families choose annually a magistrate, whom in their old language they call a Syphogrant,[1] but the newer name for them is Phylarch. Over every ten Syphogrants with their families is set a Tranibore,[2] now called the chief Phylarch. Finally the whole body of Syphogrants, in number two hundred, having sworn to choose the man whom they think most useful, by secret voting appoint as prince of the city one of the four candidates previously named to them by the people; for one is selected out of each of the four quarters of the city to be commended to the Senate. The prince holds office for life, unless he be suspected of aiming at a tyranny. The twenty Tranibores are elected annually, but not changed without good reason. The other magistrates all hold office for one year. The Tranibores consult with the prince every other day and sometimes, if need arises, oftener. They take counsel about the commonwealth, and if there be any disputes

---

[1] Probably facetiously formed from συφεοῦ γέροντες 'the old men of the sty.'

[2] Perhaps θρανιβόροι 'bench-eaters,' suggested by 'Benchers.'

between private persons—there are very few—they settle
them without loss of time. They always add to their number
two Syphogrants, and different ones every day; and it is provided that nothing concerning the commonwealth be ratified,
if it has not been discussed in the Senate three days before the
decree passes. To take counsel on matters of common interest outside the Senate or the electoral body is considered a
capital offense. They say the object of these institutions is to
prevent it being easy by a conspiracy between the prince and
the Tranibores to oppress the people by tyranny, and to
change the state of the commonwealth. Thus important matters for decision are laid before the electoral body of the
Syphogrants who, after informing their families, take counsel
together and report their decision to the Senate.[3] Sometimes
the matter is laid before the council of the whole island.
Moreover the Senate has this custom, that nothing is decided
on the same day on which it is first propounded, but that it is
put off till the next meeting,[4] and this lest anyone after hastily
uttering the idea that first came into his mouth, should afterward think more of how to defend his opinion than of
supporting what is for the good of the commonwealth, and
should prefer to jeopardize the public weal rather than risk
his reputation through a wrongheaded and misplaced shame,
fearing he may be thought to have shown too little foresight
at the first, though he should have taken care to speak with
wisdom rather than with haste in the first instance.

[3] This seems to be suggested by Tacitus *Germania* c. XI. 'On lesser matters the chiefs consult, on more important matters all the people; but
the chiefs make a preliminary consideration of affairs the decision of
which rests with the people.'
[4] Ib. 'They consult the night before, but decide next day when their
heads are clear.'

CHAPTER FOUR

OF CRAFTS AND OCCUPATIONS

Agriculture is the one pursuit which is common to all without exception, both men and women. They are all instructed in it from early years, partly by regular teaching in school, partly by being taken out into the land adjacent to the city as if for amusement, where they do not merely look on, but as opportunity arises for bodily exercise, they do the actual work. Besides agriculture which is, as I said, common to all, each is taught one particular craft as his own. This is generally either wool-working, or the preparation of flax, or masonry, or carpentry, or blacksmith's work, or silk weaving; and there is no other pursuit, which occupies any number worth speaking of. For each family makes its own clothes. These are of one pattern throughout the island, though there is a distinction for the sexes and between the married and unmarried; and they wear the same sort of clothes all their lives. The garments are comely to the eye, convenient for the movement of the body, and fit for summer and winter wear. Of the other crafts each learns one, and not the men only, but the women too. But the women, as the weaker sex, have the lighter occupations, and generally work wool and flax; to the men are committed the other more laborious crafts. As a rule each is brought up in his father's craft, for which most have a natural inclination. But if anyone is attracted to another occupation, he is transferred by adoption to a family pursuing that craft for which he has a liking, care being taken not only by his father, but by the magistrates too, that he shall be assigned to a grave and honorable householder. Moreover if anyone after being thoroughly taught one craft desires another also, the same permission is given. Having acquired both, he practices which he pleases, unless the city has more need of one than of the other. The chief and almost the only function of the Syphogrants is to see that no one sits idle, but that each applies himself zealously to his craft, yet is not wearied like a beast of burden with constant toil from early morning till late at night; for such wretchedness is worse than the life of slaves, and yet it is almost everywhere the common lot of workmen except in Utopia.[1] They divide the day and night into twenty-four equal hours, and assign only six to work, three before noon, after which they go to dinner; and after dinner, when they have rested for two hours in the afternoon, they again give three to work and finish up with supper. About 8 o'clock (counting the first hour as beginning at midday) they go to bed, and sleep claims eight hours. The intervals between the hours of work sleep and food, are left to every man's discretion, not to waste in luxury or idleness, but that the time which is free of occupation may be devoted to some other

---

[1] An Act of Parliament 1496, reenacted in 1514, provided that the hours of day laborers from March to September were to be from before 5 a.m. to between 7 and 8 p.m., with only two hours for meals; and from September to March from sunrise to sunset. In contrast with this the Utopians are only compelled to work six hours a day.

pursuit according to taste. These intervals are commonly devoted to letters and learning. For it is their custom, that public lectures are daily delivered in the early morning hours, which those only are compelled to attend who are specially chosen to devote themselves to learning. However a great number of all classes, both men and women, go to hear the lectures, some to one and some to another, according to their natural inclination. But if anyone prefer to devote this time to his craft, which is the case with many whose minds are not elevated by the contemplation of any branch of knowledge, he is not prevented, but rather commended as a useful citizen.

After supper they spend one hour in play, in summer in the gardens, in winter in the common halls in which they have their meals. There they either practice music or entertain themselves with conversation. Dicing and such foolish and pernicious games they are not even acquainted with. But there are two games which they play, not unlike chess, one a battle of numbers in which one number takes another; the other a game in which vices fight a pitched battle with virtues. In this game is exhibited very cleverly the strife of vices with one another and their concerted opposition to virtues; also what vices are the opposite of what virtues, by what strength they openly assail them and by what contrivances they indirectly attack them, by what reinforcement the virtues break the power of the vices, by what arts they frustrate their designs, and by what means the one side gains the victory.

But here, lest you be mistaken, there is one point you must examine more closely. For since they devote but six hours to work, it may be that you think the consequence is some scarcity of necessities. But so far is this from being the case, that that time is not only enough, but more than enough for a supply of all that is requisite for the necessity or the convenience of life; which you, too, will understand if you consider how large a part of the population does no work in other countries. First there are almost all women, who are half the whole, and where the women are busy, there as a rule the men are snoring in their stead. Then there is the great and idle company of priests and the so-called 'religious.' Add to them all the rich, and especially the owners of estates, who are commonly called gentlemen and noblemen. Reckon also with them their retainers, I mean that rabble of good-for-nothing swashbucklers. Finally add the lusty and sturdy beggars, who make some disease an excuse for idleness, and you will certainly find far less numerous than you had supposed those whose labor produces all the articles that men require for daily use. Now estimate how few, of these who work, are occupied in essential trades. For in a society which makes money the standard of everything, it is necessary that many crafts should be followed which are quite vain and superfluous, ministering only to luxury and licentiousness. For if the number of those who now work were distributed over only as many crafts as natural use and convenience require, in the great abundance of commodities which must then arise, the prices of them would be too low for the craftsmen to get their living by their work. But if all those who are now busied with unprofitable crafts and all the lazy and idle crowd, of whom any one now consumes as much of the fruits of other men's labors as any two of the workmen, were all set to useful occupation, you can easily see how small an allowance of time would be enough and to spare for the production of all that is required by necessity or comfort or even pleasure, provided it is genuine and natural: and the experience of Utopia makes this clear. For there in the whole city and immediate neighborhood, exemption from work is granted to no more than five hundred of the total of men and women, whose age and strength makes them fit for work. Among them the Syphogrants, though exempted by law from work, yet take no advantage of this exemption, so that by their example they may stimulate others to work. The same exemption is enjoyed by those to whom the people, persuaded by the recommendation of the priests, have given perpetual freedom from labor through a secret vote of the Syphogrants, that they may learn thoroughly various branches of knowledge. But if any of these falsifies the hopes entertained of him, he is thrust back into the ranks of the artisans; and on the other hand not seldom does it happen that an artisan so industriously employs his spare hours on learning and makes such progress by his diligence, that he is relieved of his manual labor and advanced into the class of the learned.

It is out of this class that they choose ambassadors, priests, Tranibores, and finally the king himself, whom they call in their ancient language Barzanes, but in the more modern tongue Ademus.[2] The rest of the people being neither idle nor busied with useless occupations, it is easy to reckon how much good work can be produced in a few hours. Besides what I have mentioned, there is this further convenience that in most of the necessary crafts they do not require so much work as other nations. For in the first place the building or repair of houses requires the constant labor of so many men everywhere; because what a father has built, his extravagant heir allows to fall into decay; so that what might have been kept up at small cost, his successor is obliged to re-erect at

[2] The name Barzanes occurs in Diodorus Siculus ii. 1 as that of a king of Armenia, and in Arrian Anabasis iv. 7 as that of a satrap. The name A—demus in Greek means 'without a people.'

great expense. Nay, often even when a house has cost one man a large sum, another is so fastidious that he thinks little of it, and when it is neglected, and therefore soon falls into decay, he builds another elsewhere at no less cost. But according to the careful settlement and constitution prevailing in Utopia, it seldom happens that a new site is chosen for building a house, and not merely is a remedy quickly found for actual defects, but those which threaten are averted. So with little labor houses last very long, and masons and carpenters sometimes have scarcely anything to do, except that they are set to hew timber at home, and use the time to square and prepare stone, so that if any work be required, it may the sooner be erected. In the matter of clothing, too, see how little labor is required. First, while they are at work, they are dressed carelessly in hide or skins, which last for seven years. When they go out of doors, they put on an outer garment to hide their working clothes; this is of one color through the whole island and that the natural color. So not only is much less woolen cloth needed than elsewhere, but what they have is less expensive. Linen cloth is made with less labor, and is more used. In linen cloth only whiteness, in woolen only cleanliness is considered. No store is set by fineness of thread. So it comes about that, whereas elsewhere one man is not satisfied with four or five woolen gowns of different colors and as many silk coats, and the more dainty not even with ten, in Utopia a man is content with one generally for two years. For there is no reason why he should desire more; for if he had them he would not be better fortified against the cold, or appear in the least better dressed.

Wherefore, seeing that they are all busied with useful crafts, and are satisfied with fewer products from them, it happens that when there is an abundance of commodities, sometimes they take out a great number of men to repair any of the public roads which are in bad order; and often when there is nothing of the kind to be done, they advertise that there will be fewer hours of work. For the magistrates do not keep the citizens against their will at superfluous labor; for the constitution of the state has this sole object, that so far as the public needs permit, as much time as possible should be withdrawn from the service of the body and devoted to the freedom and culture of the mind: for herein do they deem the happiness of life to consist.

CHAPTER FIVE

OF THEIR DEALINGS WITH ONE ANOTHER

But now, methinks, I must explain how the citizens behave to one another, what are the dealings of the people among themselves and what is the method of distribution of goods. Since the city consists of families, families as a rule are made up of those related by blood. For women, on arriving at maturity, when married to husbands, go into their houses. But male children and the next generation remain in the family and are subject to the oldest parent, unless he has become a dotard with old age, in which case the next oldest is put in his place. But that the city be neither depopulated nor grow beyond measure, it is provided that no family, of all the six thousand which each city apart from the surrounding district contains, shall have fewer than ten or more than sixteen adults; for of children underage no number can be fixed. This limit is easily observed by transferring those who exceed the number in larger families into those that are under the prescribed number. But when there is an increase in the whole state above the fixed limit, then they make up the deficient population of other cities. But if it chance that all over the island there has been an undue increase of population, they enroll citizens out of every city; and on the mainland nearest to them, wherever the natives have much unoccupied waste land, they found a colony, as a branch of the parent stem, under their own laws, joining with themselves the natives, wherever they are willing to dwell with them.[1] When with their consent they unite with them, the two sections easily grow into the same way of life and manners, to the great advantage of both peoples. For by their arrangements they make the land sufficient for both, which previously seemed scanty or churlish to the one. If the natives refuse to live according to their laws, they drive them out of the territory which they define for themselves; and if they resist, they fight against them; for they think it the most just cause for war, when a people which does not use its soil but keeps it void and vacant, nevertheless forbids the use and possession of it to others, who by the law of nature ought to be maintained out of it. If ever any accident so diminishes the number of any of their cities, that it cannot be made up out of other parts of the island without bringing other cities below their proper strength (this has only happened once in all the ages, when a fierce pestilence was raging), they are filled up by citizens being drafted back from the colony. For they would rather that

---

[1] Mr. Churton Collins points out that Grotius, *De Jure Belli et Pacis,* Book II. c. 2, § 17, is of opinion that there is no property 'except as concerns jurisdiction, which always continues the right of the ancient people' in waste land, which may lawfully be occupied by strangers. Puffendorf *Law of Nations,* Book III. c. 3, § 10, says there is no such right of settlement except by the consent of the original occupiers. More seems to go farther than Grotius in his 'suis ipsorum legibus,' and is obviously thinking of the Greek colonies, which fringed the coasts of the Mediterranean and Black Sea.

the colonies should perish than that any of the cities of the island should be enfeebled.

But to return to the intercourse of the citizens, the oldest, as I have said, rules the family. Wives wait on their husbands, children on their parents, and generally the younger on their elders. Every city is divided into four quarters. In the middle of each quarter is a market of all kinds of commodities. To certain houses in the marketplace the products of each family are conveyed and each kind of goods is arranged separately in storehouses. From these any father of a family seeks what he and his require, and without money or any kind of compensation carries off what he seeks. For why should anything be refused? There is a plentiful supply of all things, and there is no fear that anyone will demand more than he requires. And why should it be thought that he will demand superfluities, who is sure that he will never want for anything? For in all kinds of living creatures, fear of want causes covetousness and greed, in man pride alone, which counts it a glory to excel others by superfluous ostentation of goods; which kind of vice can have no place at all among the Utopians.

Next to the marketplaces that I have mentioned, are provision markets, to which are brought not only vegetables and fruit and bread; but also fish, and all beasts and birds that are fit for food, while places are appointed outside the city where all disease and filth may be washed away in running water. From these places the carcasses of the animals when killed are cleansed and conveyed by their slaves; for they do not allow their citizens to accustom themselves to the butchering of animals (by the practice of which they think that pity and the finer feelings of human nature are gradually killed out), nor do they allow inside the city anything dirty or unclean, for fear the air tainted by putrefaction should engender disease.

Moreover each street has spacious halls, at equal distance from each other, and each with a special name of its own. In these live the Syphogrants, and to each of them are appointed thirty families, fifteen on either side, to take their meals in common. The caterers of each hall meet at a fixed time in the market and get food according to the number of persons in each. Especial care is taken of the sick, who are looked after in public hospitals, of which they have four in the circumference of the town, a little outside the walls. These are so roomy that they may be compared to as many small towns, the purpose being both that the sick, however numerous, should not be packed too) close together in discomfort, and also that those who have got a contagious malady likely to pass from one to another, may be isolated as much as possible from the rest. These hospitals are so furnished and equipped with everything conducive to health, and such delicate and careful treatment is given by the constant attendance of expert physicians, that though no one is sent to them against his will, there is hardly anybody in the whole city who, when ill, does not prefer to be nursed there rather than at home. When the caterer for the hospitals has received food as prescribed by the physicians, then the rest is equally distributed among the halls according to the number in each, except that regard is had to the Prince, the Bishop, the Tranibores, and also to ambassadors, and all foreigners, if there be any, but these are few and seldom found. But they too, when they are there, have special furnished houses got ready for them. To these halls, at the fixed hours of dinner and supper, the whole Syphogranty assembles, summoned by a trumpet blast, except those who are sick in the hospitals or taking their meals at their own houses. But no one is forbidden to fetch food from the market to his house, after the halls have been served; for they know that this is never done without good reason. For though no one is forbidden to dine at home, yet no one does it willingly, for it is considered dishonorable; and it is foolish to have the trouble of preparing an inferior dinner when a rich and sumptuous one is ready to hand so close in a hall. In the hall all menial offices, which involve hard labor and soil the hands, are performed by slaves. But the duty of cooking and serving the meat and of arranging the whole meal is carried out by the women alone, taking turns for each family. They sit down at three or more tables according to the number of the company. The men sit with their backs to the wall, the women on the outer side, so that if any sudden trouble comes on them, such as often happens to women with child, they may rise and go to the nurses without interfering with the rows. The nurses sit separately with the infants in a room appointed for the purpose, with a fire and a supply of clean water, and with cradles provided, so that when they will, they can lay the infants down, or again take them out by the fire and undo their bindings and let them play. Each woman nurses her own offspring, unless prevented by death or disease. When that happens, the wives of the Syphogrants quickly provide a nurse and find no difficulty in doing so; for those who can do the service offer themselves with the greatest readiness, since all praise this kind of charity; and the child that is brought up looks on his nurse as his natural mother. In the nurses' rooms are all the children up to five years of age: all other children, that is all of both sexes below the age of marriage, either wait at table on their elders, or if they are not old and strong enough, stand by in absolute silence; both classes eat what is handed to them from the table, and have no other separate mealtimes. The Syphogrant and his wife sit in the middle of the high table, the place of honor, from which they have the whole company in view, for this table stands crosswise at the farthest part of the room. Alongside of them are two of the seniors, for they always sit four at a table. If there is a church in the Syphogranty, the priest and his wife sit with the Syphogrant to preside. On both sides of them sit the juniors, and next to them old men again, and so it is throughout the house that those of the same age sit together, and yet are associated with those of a different age. The reason for this practice is, they say, that the grave and reverend behavior of the old may restrain the young from wanton license of words and gestures, since nothing can be done or said at table which escapes the notice of their neighbors on either side. The courses are not served in order from the first place, but all the old men, whose places are specially marked, are first served with the best food, and then equal portions are given to the rest. But the old men at their discretion give a share to their neighbors of their dainties, when there is not enough to go round to everybody. Thus due respect is paid to seniority, and yet all have an equal advantage. They begin every dinner and supper with some reading, which is conducive to morality, but is brief so as not to be tiresome. Next the elders introduce good subjects of conversation, which must be neither too serious nor devoid of wit. But they do not take up the whole dinner with long talks, but are ready to hear the young men too, and indeed draw them out that they may try the ability and talent of each, which will show itself in the freedom of intercourse. Their dinners are somewhat short, their suppers more prolonged, because the first are followed by labor, the latter by sleep and rest; which they think to be more efficacious to wholesome digestion. No supper passes without music, nor does the repast lack sweetmeats; they burn spices, and scatter perfumes, and omit nothing that may cheer the company; for they are much given to this sort of thing, and regard no

kind of pleasure as forbidden, provided no harm comes of
it. Thus they live a common life in the city; but in the country, those who are far removed from others take their meals
at their own homes. For no family lacks any kind of food,
inasmuch as all the food which the city dwellers eat comes
from those who live in the country.

CHAPTER SIX

OF TRAVELING

Now if any conceive a desire to visit their friends who reside in another city, or to see the country itself, they easily obtain leave from their Syphogrants and Tranibores, unless when there is some good reason to prevent them. Then a party is made up and dispatched carrying a letter of the Prince, which bears witness to the granting of leave to travel, and fixes the day of their return. A carriage is granted them with a slave of the state to conduct and see to the oxen; but unless they have women in their company, they dispense with the carriage, regarding it as a burden and impediment. Throughout their journey, though they take out nothing with them, yet nothing is lacking, for they are everywhere at home. If they stay longer than a day in any place, each practices his craft, and is courteously entertained by his brethren of the same craft. If anyone gives himself leave to stray outside his limits, caught without the Prince's certificate, he is treated with contempt and brought back as a runaway and severely punished; a repetition of the offense entails the punishment of slavery. But if anyone is seized with the desire of exploring the country belonging to his own city, he is not forbidden to do so, if he obtain his father's leave and his wife's consent; but in any part of the country to which he comes he receives no food until he has finished the morning share of the day's work, or the labor that is usually performed there between dinner and supper. If he keeps to this condition, he may go where he pleases within the territory belonging to his city. For he will be just as useful to the city as if he were in it.

Now you can see, how there is nowhere any opportunity of evading work, and no pretext for idleness—no wine shop, no ale house, no house of ill fame, no opportunity of corruption, no lurking corners, no unlawful place of resort; but being under the eyes of all men they are bound either to perform the usual labors, or to be taking lawful and respectable recreation. This general fashion observed by all must of necessity lead to a provision of ample store of all things; and as this is distributed evenly among all, it follows that no one can be reduced to poverty or beggary. In the Senate of Amaurote, to which, as I said before, every city annually sends three members, as soon as it is established what article is in plenty in any particular place, and again of what there is a scarcity anywhere, they fill up the lack of one place by the superfluity of another. This they do without payment, receiving nothing in return from those to whom they give: but those who have given out of their store to any particular city, without requiring any return from it, receive what they lack from another to which they have not given anything. Thus the whole island is like a single family. But when they have made sufficient provision for themselves (which they do not consider complete until they have provided for two years to come, on account of the uncertainty of next year's crop), then they export into other countries, out of their superfluities, a great quantity of corn, honey, wool, flax, wood, cochineal and purple dye, fleeces, wax, tallow, leather, and also livestock. Of all these things they present the seventh part to the poor of that district, and sell the rest at a moderate price. By this traffic they bring into their country not only such wares as they lack themselves—and practically everything is found there but iron—but also a great quantity of silver and gold. This has lasted so long that now they have everywhere an abundance of these things, more than would be believed. And so now they care little whether they sell for ready money or appoint a future day for payment, and most frequently have outstanding debts.

But in all transactions in which payment is not made immediately, they trust not to the credit of individuals but to that of a city, legal documents being as a rule drawn up. When the day for payment has come, the city collects the money owing from private debtors and puts it into the treasury, and enjoys the use of it, until the Utopians claim payment. But for the most part they do not ask repayment; for they do not think it fair to take away a thing which is useful to people, when it is of no use to themselves. But if occasion requires that they should lend some part of it to another people, then they call in their debts; or when war is to be waged they do the same. For that one purpose they keep at home all the treasure they possess, that it may be of service to them in extreme peril or in sudden emergencies, and chiefly to hire at high rates of pay foreign mercenaries, whom they would rather jeopardize than their own citizens, being well aware that by large sums of money even their enemies themselves may be bought and sold, or set to fight one another by treachery or open warfare. For this reason they keep a vast treasure, but not as a treasure. For how they keep it, I am really quite ashamed to say, for fear that my words will not be believed; and my fears are all the more justified, as I am conscious that, had I not been there and witnessed it, I should have been with difficulty induced to believe it from another's recital. For it needs must be that in so far as a thing is unlike the manners and ways of the hearers, so far is it from obtaining their credence, though an impartial judge will perhaps wonder less, seeing that the rest of their institutions are so unlike ours, that the use of gold and silver should be adapted to their way of life rather than to ours. For as they do not use money themselves but only keep it for an emergency, which may indeed befall but possibly may never happen, in the meantime gold and silver, of which money is made, are so treated by them that no one values them more highly than their own nature deserves; and anyone can see that they are far inferior to iron in usefulness, since without iron man cannot live any more than without fire and water, but to gold and silver nature has given no use that we cannot dispense with, if the folly of men had not made them valuable because they are rare. On the other hand, like a kind and indulgent parent, she has exposed to view all that is best, like air, water and earth itself, and removed as far as possible from us all vain and unprofitable things.

So if among them these metals were kept locked up in a tower, it might be suspected that the Prince and the Council—for such is the foolish imagination of the common people—were deceiving the people by craft, and themselves deriving some benefit therefrom. Moreover, if they made them into drinking cups and other such skillful handiwork, then, if occasion arose for them all to be melted down again and applied to the pay of soldiers, they see that people will be unwilling to be deprived of what they have begun to treasure. To avoid these dangers, they have devised a means, which as it is consonant with the rest of their institutions, so is extremely unlike our own—seeing that we value gold so much, and are so careful in hoarding it—and therefore incredible except to those who have experience. For while they themselves eat and drink from earthenware and glass of fine workmanship but small value, of gold and silver they make chamber-pots and vessels of vile use not only in the common halls but in private houses. Moreover they use the same metals to make the chains and fetters which they put on their slaves.[1] Finally those who are degraded on account of some offense, have gold earrings, gold finger rings, gold chains round their necks, and gold circlets on their heads. Thus by every means in their power they make gold and silver a mark of disgrace; and thus, while other nations bear the loss of these metals with as great grief as if they had lost their own vitals, in Utopia, if ever circumstances required the removal of them, no one would feel that he had lost as much as a farthing. They also gather pearls by the seashore,[2] and on certain rocks diamonds and carbuncles too; but they do not look for them; only when they chance to find them, they polish them. With them they decorate little children, who in their early years are proud and delighted with such ornaments, but when they have got rather older and perceive that only children use these toys, they lay them aside, not from any order of their parents, but through their own feeling of shame, just as our children, when they grow up, lay aside their nuts, necklaces and dolls. And it came out

[1] Cp. Dio Chrysostom, *Oration* 79, §3. 'If it were any good to possess gold, the Ethiopians of the interior would be counted most happy; for with them gold is held in less honour than lead with us, and they say that in that country criminals are bound with stout fetters of gold.'

[2] Vespucci in his second voyage came to a people who thought nothing of gold, pearls and jewels.

most clearly at the visit of the Anemolian[3] ambassadors what opposite feelings and ideas are created by customs so different from those of other people. They came to Amaurote during my stay there, and as they came to treat of important matters, the three representatives of each city in the island had assembled before their coming. Now all the ambassadors of neighboring nations, who had previously visited Utopia, being well acquainted with the manners of the Utopians and knowing that they paid no respect to costly clothes, but looked with contempt on silk and regarded gold as a badge of disgrace, had usually come in the simplest possible dress. But the Anemolians, living farther off and having had fewer dealings with them, since they heard that in Utopia all were dressed alike and with equal simplicity, felt sure that they did not possess what they made no use of; and being more proud than wise, determined by the grandeur of their apparel to reflect the gods themselves, and by their splendid appearance to dazzle the eyes of the poor Utopians. And so the three ambassadors made a grand entry with a suite of a hundred followers, all in party-colored clothes and most of silk. The ambassadors themselves, who were noblemen at home, were arrayed in cloth of gold, with big chains of gold and gold earrings, with gold rings on their fingers, and with strings of pearls and precious stones upon their caps; in fact decked out with all those things which in Utopia were used to punish slaves, to stigmatize evil-livers or to amuse children. And so it was a sight to see how cock-a-hoop they were when they compared their grand clothing with the dress of the Utopians, who had poured out into the streets to see

[3] Anemolian is derived from the Greek word meaning 'windy.' In the prefatory matter is included a Hexastichon, attributed to Anemolius, the poet laureate of Utopia.

them pass; and on the other hand it was no less amusing to notice how much they were mistaken in their sanguine expectations, and how far they were from obtaining the consideration which they had hoped to get. For in the eyes of the Utopians, with the exception of very few, who had visited other countries, all this gay show appeared disgraceful; they therefore bowed to the lowest of the party, but took the ambassadors themselves to be slaves, because they were wearing gold chains, and passed them over without any deference whatever. Why you might have seen children, who had themselves discarded pearls and precious stones, when they saw them attached to the caps of the ambassadors, nudge their mothers and say to them: 'Look, mother, what a big rascal is still wearing pearls and jewels as if he were a little boy!' But the mother, also in earnest, would say, 'Hush, my son, I think it is one of the ambassadors' jesters.' Others would find fault with the golden chains as useless, being so slender that a slave could easily break them, or again, so loose that when he liked he could throw them off and escape scot free. When, after spending a few days there, the ambassadors saw such a quantity of gold so cheaply held and inasmuch discredit there as in honor with themselves, and moreover that more gold and silver was amassed to make the chains and leg-fetters of one runaway slave than had made up the whole array of the three of them, they were crestfallen and for shame put away all the finery with which they had made themselves so conspicuous, especially when after familiar talk with the Utopians they had learned their ways and opinions.

For the Utopians wonder that any man can take pleasure in the uncertain brightness of a tiny jewel or precious stone, when he can look at a star or the sun itself, or that anyone can be so mad as to think himself grander because he wears wool of a finer thread; and yet, however fine it be, a sheep once wore it, and yet was nothing more than a sheep all the time. They wonder, too, that gold, which in its nature is so useless, is now everywhere valued so highly, that man himself, by whom and for whose use it got this value, is held much cheaper than gold; so much so that a blockhead, who has no more wit than a post, and is as wicked as he is foolish, keeps in bondage many wise and good men, merely for the reason, that he has got hold of a great heap of gold coins. Yet if some chance or legal trick, which is as apt as chance to confound high and low, should transfer it from this great man to the lowest rascal in his household, he will surely soon pass into the retinue of his former servant, as if he were a mere appendage and accompaniment of the coins. But much more do they wonder at and abominate the madness of those, who pay almost divine honors to those rich men, to whom they neither owe anything, nor are beholden in any other respect than that they are rich; and yet they know them to be so mean and miserly that they are as sure as they can be, that of all that pile of cash, so long as the rich men live, not a penny piece will ever come their way. These and similar opinions they have derived partly from their upbringing, being brought up in a commonwealth whose institutions are far removed from folly of that kind, and partly from letters and learning. For though there are not many in each city, who are relieved from other labors and devoted to learning alone, that is to say those in whom they have detected from childhood a fine talent, first-rate wits and a disposition to all good qualities, yet all children receive a tincture of learning, and a large part of the people, men and women alike, throughout their lives, devote to learning the hours which we said were free from manual labor. They learn the various branches of knowledge in their native tongue, which is copious in vocabulary and pleasant to the ear, and a very faithful exponent of thought, being almost the same as that current in a great part of that side of the world, only that everywhere else its form is more corrupt, to different extents in different parts. Of all those philosophers, whose names are famous in our part of the world, the reputation of not a single one had reached them before our arrival; and yet in music, dialectic, arithmetic and geometry they have made almost the same discoveries as our predecessors. But as they are a match for the ancients in almost all respects, so they are far inferior to the modern logicians in invention. For they have not discovered a single one of those rules about restrictions, amplifications, and suppositions so ingeniously devised, which our children everywhere learn in the *Parva Logicalia*. Moreover, so far are they from ability to find out second intentions, that none of them has been able to conceive man in the abstract, though he be, as you know, colossal and greater than any giant, and we can point to him with our finger. But they are most expert in the courses of the stars and the movements of the celestial bodies. Moreover, they have cleverly devised instruments in different shapes, by which they have most exactly comprehended the movements and positions of the sun and moon and the other stars which are seen in their horizon. But of the agreements and discords of the planets, and all the deceitful divination by the stars, they do not even dream.[4] They forecast rain, winds and alternations of weather by certain tokens which they have perceived by long practice. But as to the causes of all these things, the flow of the sea, its saltness, in fine, the origin and nature of the heavens and the universe, they partly agree with our old philosophers, and

---

[4] More had a special dislike of astrology.

partly, as those differ from one another, so they, too, in introducing new theories disagree with them all, and yet do not in all respects agree with one another.

In that part of philosophy, which deals with morals, they discuss the same subjects as we do; they inquire into the good qualities of the soul and of the body and outward goods, and whether the name of good may be applied to all or simply belongs to the endowments of the soul. They discuss virtue and pleasure, but their chief debate is in what thing or things they are to hold that happiness consists. In this matter they seem to lean more than they should to the party that defends pleasure, since by it they define the whole or at least the chief part of human happiness. And what is more astonishing, is that they seek a defense for this sensuous doctrine from religion, which is grave and strict and usually solemn and unbending. For they never discuss happiness without joining to the philosophy that uses reasoning some principles derived from religion, without which they think reason weak and insufficient by itself for the investigation of true happiness. These principles are as follows. The soul is immortal and by the goodness of God born to felicity. After this life rewards are appointed for our virtues and good deeds, punishments for our crimes. Though these principles are matters of faith, yet they think that reason constrains them to believe and acknowledge them. But if they be removed and disallowed, they have no hesitation in saying that pleasure must be the aim of all men, to be sought by fair means or foul, and that no other opinion is tenable; only that man must take care not to let the lower pleasure interfere with the higher, nor to follow after a pleasure which will bring pain as its consequence. For to follow after a hard and painful virtue, and not only to drive away all pleasantness in life but even voluntarily to suffer pain, from which you can expect no profit (for what profit can there be, if after death you gain nothing, when you have passed your whole life unpleasantly, that is wretchedly?)—this they declare to be the extreme of madness. But as it is, they think happiness rests not in all kinds of pleasure, but only in such as are good and honorable. For to these, as to the supreme good, our nature is drawn by virtue itself (to which alone the opposite school attributes happiness). For they define virtue as a life according to nature, for which we are intended by God, and that man, they say, but follows the guidance of nature who, in desiring one thing and avoiding another, obeys the dictates of reason. Now reason first of all inflames men to a love and veneration of the Divine majesty, to which we owe both our existence and our capacity for happiness; secondly, it urges and admonishes us to lead our lives as free from care and as full of joy as possible,[5] and because of our natural fellowship with other men, to help them, too, to obtain that end. For no one was ever so sad and severe a follower of virtue and hater of pleasure, that while enforcing on you labors, watchings and discomfort, he would not at the same time bid you do your best to relieve the poverty and evils of others, and regard this as praiseworthy in the name of humanity, that one man should provide for another's health and comfort. Now if it is especially humane (and this is the virtue most peculiar to man) to relieve the misery of others and by taking away all sadness from their life, to restore them to enjoyment, that is, to pleasure, why should not nature urge everyone to do the same for himself? For either a joyous, that is a pleasurable life, is evil, in which case not only ought you to help no one to it, but you should take it away from all as being harmful and deadly, so far as you can; or else, if you

[5] Cicero *De Finibus* I. 12, 41.

not only may but are bound to praise it for others, as good, why should you not do so first of all for yourself, to whom you should show no less favor than to others? For when nature bids you to be good to others, she does not command you on the other hand to be cruel and merciless to yourself. So nature herself, say they, prescribes to us a joyous life, or in other words, pleasure as the end of all operations, and to live according to her prescription they define as virtue. But while nature calls all men to help each other to a merrier life (which certainly she does with a good reason; for no one is raised so far above the common lot of mankind as to be in his sole person the object of nature's care, seeing that she equally fosters all whom she endows with the possession of a like outward appearance), she surely bids you take constant care, not so to favor your own advantage that you cause the disadvantage of others. Therefore, they think that not only ought all bargains between private individuals to be observed, but also the common laws, which either a good king has justly proclaimed, or a nation, neither oppressed by tyranny, nor deceived by fraud, has ratified by common consent, thus giving rules for the distribution of the advantages of life, or, in other words, the means of pleasure. So long as these laws are not broken, it is wisdom to look after your own interests and piety to take care of those of the public, while to deprive others of their pleasure to secure your own, is injustice; on the other hand to take away something from yourself to give to others, is a duty of humanity and kindness, which never takes away as much advantage as it brings back: for it is compensated by the return of benefits, and the actual consciousness of the good deed; and remembrance of the love and goodwill of those whom you have benefited gives the mind more pleasure than the bodily pleasure could have been, which you have forgone. Finally—and this is brought home by religion to a mind which gladly assents—God repays in place of a brief and small pleasure great and never-ending joy. And so they think, having carefully considered and weighed the matter, that all our actions and even the virtues themselves look to pleasure as their end and true happiness. By pleasure they understand every motion and state of body or mind, in which, under the guidance of nature, a man delights to dwell. They are right in including man's natural inclinations. For just as the senses and right reason also aim at whatever is naturally pleasant, provided it is not reached by wrongdoing, does not involve the loss of something more pleasant, and is not followed by pain, so they hold that there are some things which mortals unnaturally imagine by a vain 'consensus' to be agreeable to them (as though men could change the nature of things as easily as they do their names); and all these they hold are so far from making for happiness that they are even a great hindrance to it, because they possess the minds of those in whom they have once become deep-seated, with a false idea of pleasure, so that there is no room left for true and natural delights. For there are very many things, which though of their own nature they contain no sweetness, nay the most part of them very much bitterness, yet, through the perverse attraction of evil desires, are not only regarded as the greatest pleasures but are also counted among the chief things that make life worth living. Among the class who follow this spurious pleasure, they put those whom I mentioned before,[6] who think themselves the better men, the better the clothes they wear; in which one thing they make two mistakes. For they are no less deceived in thinking their clothes better than in thinking themselves better. For if you consider the use of the

[6] Cp.

garment, why is wool of fine thread superior to that of thicker? And yet, as if it were by nature and not by their own mistake that they had the advantage, they hold their heads high, and think some extra value attaches to themselves thereby; and thus the honor, which if ill clad they would not have ventured to hope for, they require as if of right for a smarter robe; and if passed by with neglect, they are indignant. Again does it not show the same stupidity to think so much of empty and unprofitable honors? For what true and natural pleasure can the bared head or bowed knees of another give you? Will this cure the pain in your own knees, or relieve the frenzy of your own head? In this imaginary notion of pleasure men show a strange madness, who conceive themselves to be noble, and plume themselves on it and applaud themselves, because it has been their fortune to be born of ancestors, of whom a long succession has been counted rich—for that is now the only nobility—and especially rich in landed estates: and they think themselves not a whit less noble even if their ancestors have not left them an acre, or if they themselves have consumed in extravagant living what was left.

In this class, too, they count those who, as I said, dote on jewels and precious stones, and think themselves a species of gods if ever they secure a fine specimen, especially of the sort which at the period is regarded as of the highest value in their country (now it is not always and everywhere that one kind of stone is most highly prized); for they will not purchase them unless they are taken out of their gold setting and exposed to view; and not even then, until they have made the seller take an oath and give security that it is a true jewel and a true stone; so anxious are they lest a spurious stone deceive their eyes in place of a genuine one. But why should a counterfeit one give less pleasure to your sight, when your eye cannot distinguish it from the true article? Both should be of equal value to you, even as they would be to a blind man. What can be said of the men who keep superfluous wealth, to please themselves not with putting it to any use but merely with looking at it? Do they feel any real pleasure, or are they not rather cheated by an unreal pleasure? Or, of the men who have the opposite failing and put out of sight the gold, which they will never use and perhaps never see again; and in their anxiety not to lose it, lose it indeed? For what else is it to put it back in the ground, and so to deprive yourself of its use and perhaps all other men too? And yet you exult over your hidden treasure as though you were quite free from all anxiety. Yet suppose someone removed it by stealing it, and you died ten years afterwards knowing nothing of the theft, during all those ten years which you lived after the money was stolen, what did it matter to you whether it was removed or safe? In either case it was just as little use to you. Among those who indulge such senseless delights they reckon dicers (whose madness they know not by experience, but by hearsay only), moreover hunters and hawkers. For what pleasure is there, say they, in casting dice into a box, which you have done so often, that if there had been some pleasure in it, weariness would by now have arisen from the habitual practice? Or what agreeableness can there be and not rather disgust, in hearing the barking and howling of dogs? Or what greater sensation of pleasure is there, when a dog chases a hare, than when a dog runs after a dog? For the same thing happens in both cases; there is running in both, if speed gives you pleasure. But if you are attracted by the hope of slaughter and the expectation of a creature being mangled under your eyes, it ought rather to inspire pity, when you behold a poor, weak, timid and innocent hare torn to pieces by a strong, fierce and cruel dog. And so the people of Utopia have passed the whole exercise of hunting over to their butchers, as unworthy of free men, and as I said before, they make their slaves butchers; for they regard hunting as the meanest part of the butcher's craft, and the other departments of it as much more useful and honorable, seeing that they do much more good and only kill animals from necessity, while the hunter seeks nothing but pleasure from the killing and mangling of a poor animal. This desire of looking on at bloodshed in the case of beasts they think either arises from a cruel disposition, or through the constant practice of such savage pleasure degenerates into cruelty. These, therefore, and all similar pursuits, which are countless, though common people regard them as pleasures, yet they hold positively to have nothing to do with real pleasure, since there is nothing naturally agreeable in them. For the fact that they commonly inspire a feeling of enjoyment (which seems to be the function of pleasure) does not alter this opinion; for the enjoyment does not arise from the nature of the thing, but from their own perverse habit, by reason of which they take what is bitter for sweet; just as pregnant women by their vitiated taste think pitch and tallow sweeter than honey. Yet it is impossible for any man's judgment, depraved either by disease or habit, to change the nature of pleasure any more than of anything else.

The pleasures which they admit as genuine they divide into various classes, some being of the soul, and others of the body. To the soul they ascribe intelligence and the delight which is bred of contemplation of the truth; and to this is added the pleasant recollection of a well-spent life, and the sure hope of happiness to come. Bodily pleasure they divide into two parts. The first is that which fills the sense with perceptible sweetness, which sometimes comes by the renewing of those parts which have been emptied by our natural heat; for they are restored by food and drink; sometimes this agreeable sensation comes, when the overloaded body is relieved by evacuation, when either we relieve nature, or have sexual connection, or relieve the itching of some part by rubbing or scratching. But sometimes pleasure arises, not in process of restoring anything that our members lack, nor of taking away anything that causes pain, but from something which tickles and moves our senses with a secret force but with a palpable motion and so draws them to itself, such as that pleasure which is engendered by music. The second part of bodily pleasure, they say, is that which consists in a calm and harmonious state of the body, that is when a man's health is not interrupted by any disorder. For this, if assailed by no pain, gives delight of itself, though there be no pleasure applied from without. For though it is less obvious and less perceptible by the sense than the coarser desire of eating and drinking, yet nonetheless many hold it to be the greatest pleasure. Almost all the Utopians regard it as great, and practically the basis and foundation of all pleasures; for it alone can make the state of life peaceful and desirable, and without it there is no place left for any pleasure; for being without pain, when health is absent, they regard as insensibility rather than pleasure. They have long ago rejected the position of those who held that a state of tranquil and stable health (for this question, too, has been actively discussed among them) was not to be counted as a pleasure,[7] because they said its presence could not be felt except through some opposite emotion. But on the other hand they now almost all agree that health is above all things conducive to pleasure. For

[7] Cp. Plato *Republic* IX. 583–7; *Gorgias* 494–5; Cicero *De Finibus*, Book I.

since in disease there is pain, which is the bitter enemy of pleasure, no less than disease is of health, why should not pleasure be found in the tranquility of health? For they think that it is of no importance whether you say that disease is pain or that pain is disease, for it comes to the same thing either way. For if you hold that health is either a pleasure itself or the necessary cause of pleasure, as fire is of heat, in both ways it results that those who have settled health cannot be without pleasure. Besides, while we eat, say they, what is that but health, which had begun to be impaired, fighting against hunger with the assistance of food? And while it gradually gains strength, the very progress to the usual vigor supplies the pleasure, by which we are thus restored. Shall the health, which delights in conflict, not rejoice when it has gained the victory? And, when at length it has successfully acquired its former strength, which was its sole object throughout the conflict, shall it forthwith become insensible and not recognize nor embrace its own good? For when it is said that health cannot be felt by the senses, they think that is quite false. Who when awake, say they, does not feel that he is in health, except he who is not? Who is fast bound with such insensibility or lethargy, that he does not confess that health is pleasant and delightful to himself? But what is delight except pleasure under another name? First of all therefore they cling to and value the pleasures of the mind, which they regard as of first-rate importance, and of these the greater part they hold to arise from the exercise of virtues and the consciousness of a good life. Of all the pleasures which the body supplies, they give the palm to health; for the delight of eating and drinking, and anything that gives the same kind of enjoyment, they think desirable, but only for the sake of health. For such things are not pleasant in themselves, but only in so far as they resist the secret assaults of ill health. And so as a wise man should rather pray that he may escape disease than desire a remedy for it, and rather drive out pain than summon a consolation to his aid, so it would be better not to require this kind of pleasure, than to be eased of pain.

But if a man think that felicity consists in this kind of pleasure, he must admit that he will be in the greatest happiness, if a life falls to his lot, which is spent in perpetual hunger, thirst, itching, eating, drinking, scratching and rubbing; and who does not see that this is not only disgusting but pitiable? These pleasures are surely the lowest of all as being most adulterated, for they never occur unless they are coupled with the pains which are their opposites. Thus with the pleasure of eating, hunger is combined and on no fair terms; for the pain is the stronger, and lasts longer, for it comes into existence before the pleasure and does not end until the pleasure dies with it. So such pleasures they hold should not be highly valued except in so far as they are necessary. Yet they enjoy even these and gratefully acknowledge the kindness of mother nature, which even with coaxing sweetness allures her offspring to that which of necessity they must constantly do. For in what discomfort should we have to live if, like other sicknesses which less frequently assail us, so too, these daily diseases of hunger and thirst had to be expelled by bitter poisons and drugs? Beauty, strength and nimbleness, these as special and pleasant gifts of nature, they gladly value. Nay, even those pleasures, which enter by the ears, eyes and nose, which nature designed to be peculiarly characteristic of man (for no other kind of living creature either takes in the fairness and form of the universe, or is affected by the pleasantness of smell, except for distinction of food, or distinguishes concordant and discordant intervals of sound), these, too, I say, they follow after, as pleasant relishes of life. But in all these they make this limitation, that the less is not to interfere with the greater, and pleasure is not to produce pain; and the latter they think a necessary consequence, if the pleasure is base. But to despise the grace of established beauty, to impair the strength of the body, to turn nimbleness into sloth, to exhaust the body and injure the health by fasting, and to reject all the other pleasant gifts of nature (unless when a man neglects these advantages to himself in providing more zealously the good of others or of the commonwealth, in return for which toil he expects a greater pleasure from God; in all other cases for a vain shadow of goodness, to no man's profit, to deal hardly with himself, even that he may more easily bear the adversity which may never come), this they think is extreme madness and a sign of a mind which is cruel to itself and ungrateful to nature, to whom he disdains to be indebted and therefore renounces all her benefits.

This is their view of virtue and pleasure, and they believe that human reason cannot attain to any truer view, unless revealed religion inspires a man with something more holy. Whether in this they are right or wrong, time does not permit us now to examine, nor is it necessary; for we have taken upon ourselves only to describe their principles, and not also to defend them.[8] But of this I am sure, that whatever you think of these opinions, there is nowhere in the world a more excellent people nor a happier state. They are active and nimble of body, and stronger than you would expect from their stature, which is, however, not dwarfish. And though they have not a very fertile soil nor a very wholesome climate, they protect themselves against the atmosphere by temperate living and make up for the defects

---

[8] More carefully guards himself against ecclesiastical censure.

of the land by diligent labor; so that nowhere in the world is there a more plentiful supply of corn and cattle, or are men's bodies more tenacious of life and subject to fewer diseases. And so you may behold not only the usual agricultural labors performed there, whereby the naturally churlish soil is improved by art and industry, but also how a whole forest has been uprooted in one place by the labors of the people, and planted in another. Herein they were thinking not so much of abundance as of transport, that they might have wood more close to the sea, or rivers, or the cities themselves. For it takes less labor to convey grain to a distance by land than timber.

The people in general are easygoing and good tempered, skillful with their hands; they enjoy rest but do their share of manual labor, when occasion requires, though at other times they are not fond of it, for they are unwearied in their devotion to mental study.

When they had heard from us about the literature and learning of the Greeks (for in Latin there was nothing apart from history and poetry, of which it seemed likely that they would much approve), they were extremely desirous that we would teach them the language and instruct them in Greek literature. We began, therefore, to read to them, more at first that we should not seem to refuse the trouble, than that we expected any result. But after a little progress, their diligence made us feel sure that our labors would not be bestowed in vain. For they began so easily to imitate the shapes of the letters and so readily to pronounce the words, so quickly to learn by heart, and so faithfully to reproduce what they learned, that it was a perfect wonder to us; though of course the greater part of them were scholars picked for their ability, and of mature years, who undertook to learn their tasks not only of their own free will but by order of the Senate. So in less than three years they were perfect in the language and able to read good authors, without any difficulty except for faulty texts.

I imagine they got hold of Greek literature more easily because it was closely allied to their own. I suspect that their race was derived from the Greek, because their language, which in other respects resembles the Persian, retains some traces of Greek in the names of their cities and magistrates. When about to go on my fourth voyage, I put on board in place of wares to sell, a fairly large bundle of books, having quite made up my mind never to return rather than to come back soon. So they have received from me most of Plato's works, almost all Aristotle's, also Theophrastus 'On Plants,' which I regret to say is imperfect in parts. For during the voyage the book was left lying about, and an ape found it, and in wanton sport tore out and destroyed several pages in various parts of the book. Of grammarians they have only Lascaris, for I did not take Gaza with me, and no lexicographer but Hesychius and Dioscorides. They are very fond of the works of Plutarch, and they delight in Lucian's sprightliness and wit. Of the poets they have Aristophanes, Homer and Euripides, and Sophocles in the small Aldine type: of the historians Thucydides and Herodotus and Herodian too. In medicine my companion, Tricius Apinatus,[9] had brought with him some small treatises of Hippocrates, and the *Microtechne* of Galen, to which books they attribute great value. For though there is scarcely any nation that needs medicine less, yet nowhere is it held in greater honor; for they regard the knowledge of it as one of the finest and most useful parts of philosophy. For when by the help of this philosophy they

---

[9] Martial xiv. 1, 7. '*Sunt apinae tricaeque et si quid vilius istis,*' i.e., trifles and bagatelles.

search out the hidden secrets of nature, they think that not only do they get great pleasure in doing so but also win the approval of the Author and Maker of all things. They think that HE, like all artificers, set forth the visible mechanism of the world as a spectacle for man, whom alone HE made capable of appreciating such a wonderful thing, and therefore HE prefers a careful and diligent beholder and admirer of His work to one who like a brute beast without sense or motion passes by so great and wonderful a spectacle. Thus the wits of the Utopians, trained in all learning, are exceedingly apt at the invention of arts which promote the advantage and convenience of life. Two, however, they owe to us, the art of printing and the manufacture of paper, though not entirely to us, but to a great extent to themselves; for when we showed them the Aldine printing in paper books, and talked about the material of which paper is made and the art of printing, (though I cannot say we explained it, for none of us was expert in either art), they promptly and with great acuteness guessed how it was done, and though previously they wrote only on skins, bark and papyrus, from this time they attempted to manufacture paper and print letters. Their first attempts were not very successful, but by frequent experiment they soon mastered both, so that if they had copies of Greek authors, they would have no lack of books. But at present they have nothing more than I have mentioned, but by printing books they have increased their stock to many thousand copies.

Whoever comes to their country on a tour of sightseeing, if he is recommended by any special intellectual endowment, or through long travel acquainted with many countries, is sure of a welcome, for they delight in hearing what is going on in every country. But few come to them in the way of trade. For what could they bring except iron, or gold and silver, which they would rather take back home with them? And as to articles of export, the Utopians think it wiser to carry them out of the country themselves than to let others come and fetch them, that so they may find out more information about foreign nations, and not lose by disuse their skill in navigation.

CHAPTER SEVEN

OF SLAVES, ETC.

They do not make slaves of prisoners in war, except it be a war waged by themselves, nor of the sons of slaves, nor of anyone whom they could acquire from bondage in other countries; but their slaves are either such as are enslaved in their own country for heinous crimes, or have been condemned to death elsewhere for some offense; and the greater number of their slaves are of this latter kind. For they bring away many of them; sometimes they buy them cheaply; but often they ask for them and get them for nothing. These classes of slaves they keep not only continually at work, but also in chains, treating their own countrymen with greater harshness, as being more hopeless and deserving of more exemplary punishment, because having had such a good education to a virtuous life they could not be restrained from crime. There is also another class of slaves; for sometimes a poor laborer voluntarily exchanges drudgery in another country for slavery in Utopia. These are well treated, and except that they have rather more labor assigned to them, are used almost as gently as citizens. If anyone wishes to depart, which seldom happens, they do not detain him against his will or send him away empty handed.

The sick, as I said,[1] are very lovingly cared for, nothing being omitted which may restore them to health, whether in the way of medicine or diet. Those who are suffering from incurable disease they console by sitting and conversing with them and applying all possible alleviations. But if a disease is not only incurable but also distressing and painful without any cessation, the priests and the magistrates[2] exhort the man, since he is now unequal to all the duties of life and by living beyond the time of his death is a burden to himself and a distress to others, to make up his mind not to foster disease and plague any longer, nor hesitate to die, now that life has become torture to him, but relying on good hope, to free himself from life which has become bitter as from a prison or from the rack, or else voluntarily to permit others to free him; in this he will act wisely, since by death he will put an end not to enjoyment but to torture; and since he will in doing so obey the counsels of the priests, who are the interpreters of God's will, it will be a pious and devout action. Those who have been convinced by these arguments, either starve themselves to death, or being put to sleep are released without the sensation of dying. But they do not make away with anyone against his will; nor in such a case do they relax at all their attendance upon him. They believe that to die, when it is sanctioned by authority, is honorable; but if anyone commits suicide without having

[1] Cp. Ch. V.

[2] Plato (*Laws* IX. 873) while strongly condemning suicide, seems to allow it in the case of an incurable and painful disease; Val. Max. II. 6, says, 'The Council at Marseilles provided hemlock for those who satisfied them of their reasons for dying.'

obtained the consent of priests and council, they deem him unworthy of fire or earth, and his body is ignominiously thrust into a marsh without proper burial.'[3]

Women are not allowed to marry till eighteen; men not till they are four years older. If the man or the woman is convicted of clandestine intercourse before marriage, he or she is severely punished, and such are forbidden to marry altogether, unless the Prince's pardon remits their guilt; but the father and mother of the family, in whose house the offense was committed, incur great disgrace, as having been neglectful in doing their parts. The reason why they punish this offense so severely, is that they foresee that unless all are restrained from promiscuous intercourse, few will contract the marriage tie, in which the whole married life must be spent with one companion, and all the vexations and troubles that are incidental to it must be patiently borne. In choosing mates they favor seriously and strictly a custom which seemed to us very foolish, and extremely ridiculous. For the woman, whether maiden or widow, is shown naked to the suitor by a worthy and respectable matron, and similarly the suitor is presented naked before the maiden by a discreet man.[4] We laughed at this custom and condemned it as foolish; but they on the other hand marveled at the notable folly of other nations, who in buying a pony, where it is only a question of a little money, are so cautious that though it is almost bare they will not buy until they have taken off the saddle and removed all the harness, for fear some sore may be concealed under these coverings, and yet in choosing

---

[3] Tacitus *Germania* 12, 1, 'The coward, the recreant, the man stained with abominable vices, is plunged into the mire of a morass with a hurdle put over him.'

[4] Plutarch (*Lycurgus*, c. 14) seems to have suggested this idea to More.

a wife, when pleasure or disgust will follow them all their lives in consequence, they are so careless, that while all the rest of her body is covered with clothes, they estimate the value of the whole woman from a single handsbreadth of her, the face only being visible, and take her to themselves not without great danger of their agreeing ill together, if something afterwards gives offense to them. For all men are not so wise as to regard the character of the woman only, and even in the marriages of wise men bodily attractions are no small enhancement to the virtues of the mind. Certainly such foul deformity may be hidden beneath these coverings, that it may quite alienate a man's mind from his wife, when bodily separation is no longer lawful. If such a deformity arise by chance after the marriage has been contracted, each must bear his own fate; but beforehand the law ought to protect him from being entrapped by guile. This provision was the more necessary, because the Utopians are the only people in that part of the world who are satisfied with one wife, and matrimony is seldom broken except by death, unless it be for adultery or intolerable offensiveness of disposition.

For when one or the other party is thus offended, leave is obtained of the Council to take another mate, while the rejected lives a life of disgrace and perpetual celibacy. But they think it undesirable to put away a wife who is in no way to blame, because some bodily drawback has befallen her; for they think it cruel that anyone should be abandoned when most in need of comfort, and that old age will thus only have a weak and unreliable protection, though it both entails disease and is a disease itself. But it sometimes happens, that when a married couple do not agree in their dispositions, and both find others with whom they hope they would live more agreeably, they separate by mutual consent and contract fresh unions, but not without the sanction of the Council, which allows of no divorce, until the members of it and their wives have carefully gone into the case. Even then they do not readily consent, because they know that it is a very great drawback to cementing the affection of married couples, if they have before them the easy hope of a fresh union. Breakers of the conjugal tie are punished by the strictest form of slavery. If both parties were married, the injured parties, with their consent, are divorced from their adulterous mates and coupled together, or else allowed to marry whom they like. But if one of the injured parties continue to feel affection for so undeserving a mate, it is not forbidden that the marriage shall continue in force, if the party is willing to accompany and share the labor of the other who has been condemned to slavery. Sometimes it happens that the penitence of the one and the dutiful assiduity of the other move the compassion of the Prince and win back their liberty; but a repetition of the same offense involves the penalty of death. For other offenses there is no law prescribing any fixed penalty, but according to its atrocity or contrariwise, the punishment is appointed by the Council. Husbands chastise their wives, and parents their children, unless the offense is so monstrous, that it is to the advantage of public morality that the punishment should be inflicted by the community. Generally the worst offenses are punished by slavery, since this prospect is just as formidable to the criminal, and they think it more advantageous to the state than if they make haste to put the offenders to death and get them out of the way; for their labor is more profitable than their death, and the example lasts longer to deter others from like crimes.[5]

---

[5] More may have been thinking of Herodotus II, 137, where it is said that Sabakos, the Ethiopian conqueror of Egypt, substituted for the death penalty the labor of throwing up earthworks to defend the cities.

But if they rebel and kick against this treatment, they are thereupon put to death, like untamable beasts that cannot be restrained by prison or fetter. But if they are patient, they are not entirely deprived of all hope; for when tamed by long misery, if they show such penitence as testifies that they are more sorry for their sin than for their punishment, then sometimes by the prerogative of the Prince, and sometimes by the resolution of the people, their slavery is either lightened or remitted altogether. To tempt another to debauchery is no less punishable than the act itself: for in all offenses the deliberate and avowed attempt is counted equal to the deed; for they think that failure ought not to benefit one whose will was to succeed.

They are very fond of jesters. It is a great disgrace to treat them with insult, but there is no prohibition against deriving pleasure from their fooling, since they think this is of great benefit to the jesters themselves. If anyone is so stern and morose that he is not amused with anything they do or say, they do not entrust him with the care of a fool, for fear that he may not treat him with sufficient indulgence, as he would be of no use nor even entertainment, which is their sole faculty. To deride a man for a deformity or the loss of a limb, is counted as base and disfiguring not to the man who is laughed at but to him that laughs, who foolishly upbraids a man with something as if it were a fault, which it was not in his power to avoid. While they think it a sign of a poor and feeble mind not to preserve natural beauty, it is, in their judgment, disgraceful insolence to help it out by painting the skin. For experience shows them how no elegance of outward form recommends wives to husbands as much as honorable and deferential behavior: while some are attracted by beauty alone, love is never retained except by virtue and obedience. Not merely do they discourage crime by punishment, but they offer honors and rewards to incite men to good deeds. Thus they set up in the market-place statues to great men who have done conspicuous service to the commonwealth, as a record of good deeds, and that the glory of ancestors may be to their descendants a spur and stimulus to virtue. He who solicits votes to obtain any office, is deprived of the hope of ever filling any whatever. They live together in affection and goodwill; for no magistrate is haughty or formidable; they are called fathers and show that character; honor is paid them willingly, as it should be, and is not exacted from the unwilling. The Prince himself is not distinguished from others by a robe or a crown, but by carrying a handful of corn, just as the mark of the Bishop is the wax candle carried before him.

They have very few laws; people so trained, need but few.[6] The chief fault they find with other people is that they have almost innumerable books of laws and commentaries on them which yet are not sufficient; for they themselves think it most unfair that any man should be bound by laws, which are too numerous to be read through, or too obscure to be understood by any. Moreover they absolutely banish from the country all advocates, who cleverly handle cases and cunningly argue legal points; for they think it a good thing that every man should plead his own cause, and say the same to the judge, as elsewhere he would tell his counsel. Thus there will be less circumlocution, and the truth is more easily elicited, when a man who has not been taught by a lawyer to deceive conducts his own case, and the judge cleverly weighs each statement and assists the more untutored

[6] Tacitus *Annals* III, 27, 'laws were most numerous when the common-wealth was most corrupt.' *Germania* 19, 'there good habits are more effectual than good laws elsewhere.'

wits to defeat the accusations of the crafty. That these advantages should be secured in other countries, is difficult owing to the mass of extremely complicated laws. With them each man is expert in law. For, as I said, they have very few laws, and in their opinion the justice of a law is dependent on the obviousness of its interpretation. For all laws, so they say, are published only that each man may be reminded of his duty, but whereas the more refined and recondite interpretation of the law reminds only very few (for there are few who can arrive at it), the more simple and obvious sense of the laws is open to all; otherwise what difference would it make for the common people, who are the most numerous and also most in need of instruction, whether you framed no law at all or when framed you interpreted it in such a sense, as no one could elicit except by great ingenuity and long argument? Now the coarse wit of the common people cannot attain to the meaning of such laws, nor can their lives be long enough, seeing that they are wholly occupied in getting a living. These virtues of the Utopians have stimulated their neighbors who are free and independent (for many of them the Utopians have long ago delivered from the tyrants who oppressed them) to obtain magistrates from them, some for a year, and others for five years. On the expiration of their office they escort them home with all honor and eulogy, and bring back with them their successors. Certainly these nations make very good and beautiful provision for their commonwealths; for since it depends on the character of their magistrates, whether they prosper or are ruined, of whom could they have made a wiser choice than of those who cannot be drawn from the path of honor by any bribe (since it is no good to them as they will shortly return home) and, as they are strangers to the citizens, cannot be influenced either by partiality or animosity toward any? These two evils, favoritism and avarice, wherever they influence the decisions of judges, instantly destroy all justice, that strongest sinew of a commonwealth. The people who fetch their magistrates from Utopia, are called allies by them; the name of friend is reserved for those whom they have themselves benefited. Treaties which all other nations so often conclude, break and again renew, they never make with any nation. What is the use of a treaty, say they, as though nature did not sufficiently of herself bind one man to another, and if a man regard not her, can one suppose he will think anything of words? They are led to this opinion chiefly because in those parts of the world treaties and covenants between Princes are not observed with much good faith.[7] In Europe, however, and especially in those parts where the faith and religion of Christ prevails, the majesty of treaties is everywhere holy and inviolable, and this arises partly through the justice and goodness of kings, and partly through their reverence and fear of Popes, who, as they undertake nothing themselves which they do not most conscientiously perform, so command all other rulers by all means to abide by their promises, and compel the recalcitrant by pastoral censure and severe reproof. To be sure they were right in thinking it a most disgraceful thing, that those who are specially called the faithful, should not faithfully adhere to their treaties.

[7] The bitter irony of More seems to be aimed at the Partition Treaty between Ferdinand of Spain and Louis XII to divide the kingdom of Naples between them in 1500, the desertion of the French by Julius II in 1510, when he formed the Holy League, and the dissolution of that League in 1514. The whole life of Francis I, who had not been quite two years on the throne when the Utopia was published, was to add point to More's words.

But in that New World, which is almost as far removed by the Equator from ours as their character and life are different, there is no reliance on treaties. For the more numerous and binding the ceremonies with which a treaty is tied and bound, the more quickly is it dissolved; they find some quibble as to the meaning of words, which sometimes they cunningly devise of set purpose, so that they can never be held by such strong bonds that they cannot somehow escape from them and break both the league and their faith. If this cunning, nay fraud and deceit, were found out to have occurred in the contracts of individuals, with great disdain they would exclaim against it as sacrilegious and meriting the gallows, though the very same men would boast themselves as the authors of such advice when given to kings. So it comes that men think either that all justice is only a low and plebeian virtue which is far below the majesty of kings, or at least that there are two forms of it: one which goes on foot and creeps on the ground, only fit for the common sort and bound by many chains, so that it can never overstep its barriers; the other the virtue of kings, which as it is more august than that of ordinary folk, is also far freer, so that everything is permitted to it except that which it does not want. The manners of kings who keep their covenants so badly are, I suppose, the reason why the Utopians make none; perhaps if they lived here, they would change their mind. But they think, even though leagues be faithfully observed, it is a pity that the custom of making them at all has grown up. For the result is (as though nations which are divided by the slight interval of a hill or a river were joined by no natural bond)[8] men think themselves born adversaries

---

[8] More is thinking of the Cheviots and the Tweed between England and Scotland.

and enemies of one another, and that they are right in aiming at the destruction of each other except in so far as treaties prevent it; nay even when treaties are made, friendship does not grow up, but the license of freebooting continues, insofar as, for lack of skill in drawing up the treaty, no sufficient precaution to prevent this was included in the compact. But the Utopians, on the other hand, think that no one who has done you no harm should be accounted an enemy, that the fellowship which nature creates takes the place of a league, and that men are better and more firmly joined together by goodwill than by covenants, by affection than by words.

CHAPTER EIGHT

OF WARFARE

War, as a thing only fit for beasts, and yet not practiced by any kind of beasts so constantly as by man, they regard with utter loathing, and contrary to the fashion of almost all nations they count nothing so inglorious as glory obtained in war; and so, though men and women alike constantly exercise themselves in military training, on fixed days, lest they should be unfit for war when need requires, yet they do not lightly undertake it, unless it be either to protect their own territory or drive an invading enemy out of their friends' country, or when in pity for a nation oppressed by tyranny they seek to deliver them by force of arms from the yoke and bondage of a tyrant, a course prompted merely by human sympathy. Though they oblige their friends with help, not always indeed to defend them, but sometimes also to avenge and requite injuries previously done to them, they only do it if they are consulted before any step is taken, and recommend that war should be declared only after they have approved the cause and demand for restitution has been made in vain. This final step they take, not only when a hostile inroad has carried off booty, but much more fiercely, when merchants who come from the country of their friends have to undergo an unjust accusation under the color of justice in any other country, either on the pretext of unjust laws or by the distortion of good laws. Such was the origin of the war, which the Utopians waged a little before our time on behalf of the Nephelogetes against the Alaopolitans.[1]

Some traders of the Nephelogetes suffered a wrong, as they thought, under pretense of law, but whether right or wrong, it was avenged by a fierce war. To this war the resources of neighboring nations were brought in to assist the power and intensify the rancor of both sides, till flourishing nations had either been shaken or overthrown, and the troubles that arose were only ended by the surrender and subjection of the Alaopolitans; these yielded themselves to the rule of the Nephelogetes (the Utopians were not fighting for their own interest), a people who, when the Alaopolitans were prosperous, were not in the least comparable to them in strength.

So severely do the Utopians punish wrongs done to their friends, even in money matters. But it is not so when the wrongs are done to themselves. When defrauded of their goods anywhere, if there be no personal violence done, their anger does not go farther than the interruption of trade with that nation, until satisfaction be made. Not that they care less for their citizens than for their friends, but they are more annoyed when their friends suffer pecuniary loss than when this happens to themselves, because their friends' traders suffer severely by the loss, as it falls on their own private property, but their own citizens lose nothing but what comes from the common stock and what was plentiful

[1] Nephelogetes 'children of the mist'; Alaopolitans 'inhabitants of the city of the blind,' names coined from Greek.

and superfluous at home, or else it would not have been exported; and thus the loss is not felt by any individual. Therefore, they think it too cruel to avenge the loss by the death of many, when the disadvantage of the loss affects neither the life nor the subsistence of any of their own people. But if any Utopian anywhere is wrongfully disabled or killed, whether the fault is due to a foreign government or individual, they first ascertain the facts by an embassy; and then if the guilty persons are not surrendered, they cannot be appeased, but forthwith declare war. If the guilty persons are surrendered, they are punished either with death or enslavement. They not only regret but are ashamed of a victory that has cost much bloodshed, thinking that it is folly to purchase wares, however precious, too dear; but if the enemy are overcome and crushed by stratagem and cunning, they boast beyond measure and celebrate a public triumph over the success and put up a trophy in token of victory, for they boast[2] themselves as having acted valiantly and showed manly prowess, when their victory is such as no animal, but only man could have won, being due to strength of mind, for by strength of body, say they, bears, lions, boars, wolves, dogs and other wild beasts are wont to fight; most of them are superior to us in strength and spirit, but they are all inferior in forethought and wit.

Their one and only object in war is to secure that which they demanded beforehand and failed to obtain; if they had obtained it they would not have fought; or else if that be out of the question, they require such severe punishment of

[2] More combines the Roman triumphal procession with the Greek 'trophy' or monument set up on the spot where the enemy was routed. The idea of rejoicing when the enemy was overcome by stratagem he probably derived from Plutarch *Instituta Laconica*, c. 25.

those on whom they lay the blame, that for the future they may be afraid to attempt anything of the sort. These are their chief interests, which they set about promptly yet taking more care to avoid danger than to win glory or honor. The moment war is declared, they arrange that simultaneously a number of placards, fortified by their own public seal, should be set up secretly in the most prominent spots of the enemies' territory, and herein they promise large rewards to anyone who will kill the King of their enemies, and further offer smaller sums, but those considerable, for the heads of the individuals whose names they specify in the same proclamations, these being the men whom, next to the King himself, they regard as responsible for the hostile measures taken against them. Whatever reward they fix for the man who kills any of these persons, they double for him who brings any of them alive; nay, they actually offer the same rewards with a guarantee of their personal security to those whose names occur in the proclamation, if they will turn against their fellows.[3]

So it soon comes about that their enemies suspect everyone outside, and neither trust nor are loyal to one another, and are in a state of utter panic and no less peril. For it is known that it has often happened that many of them, and especially the King himself, have been betrayed by those in whom they had placed implicit trust; so easily do bribes incite men to commit any crimes. Thus they are boundless in their offers of reward; remembering what a risk they invite the man to run, they take care that the greatness of the peril is outweighed by the extent of the rewards; thus they promise and faithfully pay down not only an immense amount of gold, but also landed property in freehold,

---

[3] Henry VIII's intrigues in Scotland are here plainly referred to.

bringing in a great income in secure places in the territory of friends. This habit of bidding for and purchasing an enemy, which is elsewhere condemned as the cruel act of a base and degenerate nature, they think reflects great credit on their wisdom, for thus they bring to a conclusion great wars without any battle at all; and also on their humanity and mercy, because by the death of a few guilty people they purchase the lives of many harmless persons, who would have fallen in battle both on their own side and on that of the enemy; for they are as sorry for the common soldiers of the enemy as for their own, knowing that they do not go to war of their own accord, but are driven to it by the madness of kings.

If this plan does not succeed, they sow the seeds of dissension broadcast and foster strife by leading the brother of the King or one of the noblemen to hope that he may obtain the throne.[4]

If internal strife dies down, then they stir up the neighbors of their enemies and set them by the ears, by reviving some forgotten claims to dominion such as kings have always at their disposal, and promising their own assistance for the war. But while they supply money liberally, they are very chary of sending their own citizens, whom they hold singularly dear, regarding each other as of such value, that they would not care to exchange any of their own people for the king of the opposite party. As to gold and silver, since they keep it all for this one use, they pay it out without any reluctance, for they would live just as well if they spent it all. Moreover, in addition to the riches which they keep at home, they have also a vast treasure abroad, in that many nations, as I said before,[5] are in their debt.

[4] Again an allusion to the intrigues of Henry VIII in Scotland.
[5] Cp. Chapter VI.

Thus they hire and send to fight soldiers from all parts, but especially from the country of the Zapoletes.[6] These people live five hundred miles to the east of Utopia, and are rough, boorish and brave, preferring their own woods and rugged mountains, among which they are bred. They are a hardy race, capable of enduring heat, cold, and hard work, entirely without any refinement of culture, and not skilled in husbandry, careless about the houses they live in or the clothes they wear, and only occupied with their flocks and herds. To a great extent they live by hunting and plunder. They are born for warfare and zealously seek an opportunity for fighting, which, when they find, they eagerly embrace, and leaving the country in great force, they offer themselves at a cheap rate to anyone needing fighting men. The only art of living they know is that by which they seek their deaths. They fight strenuously and loyally for those from whom they receive their pay. But they bind themselves for no fixed period, but take sides in such a way that the next day when higher pay is offered them by the enemy they take his side, and then the day after, if a little more is offered to tempt them back, return to the side they took at first. Seldom does a war arise in which there are not many of them in both armies, so it is a daily occurrence that those connected by ties of blood and those who were hired on the same side and so became very intimate with one another, soon afterwards

[6] 'Ready to sell themselves.' More means the Swiss, who were prominent as mercenaries in the Italian wars of this period. They fought against each other, for and against Ludovico Sforza, Duke of Milan. In 1500 they went over to the French and fought for Louis XII. In 1513 they helped the Pope to drive the French out of Italy. After their defeat at Marignano, Pace went to Switzerland to secure their services for Henry VIII against France.

are separated into two hostile forces and meet in battle. Then with fierce animosity, forgetting both kinship and friendship, they stab each other and are driven to destroy one another for no other reason than that they are hired by opposing kings for a small sum, of which they take such careful account that they are readily induced to change sides by the addition of a penny to their daily rate of pay. So quickly have they developed a habit of covetousness, which profits them not one whit; for what they get by exposing their lives, they spend instantly in riotous living and wretchedness. This people will fight for the Utopians against any enemies whatsoever, because they are hired at a rate higher than they could get anywhere else. The Utopians, just as they seek good men to use, so enlist these bad men to abuse. For when need requires, they send them under the tempting bait of big promises into great peril, whence a large proportion never returns to claim their fulfillment; but the survivors are honestly paid what has been promised them, to incite them again to like deeds of daring. For they do not care how many of them they lose, thinking that they would be benefactors to the whole human race, if they could relieve the world of all the dregs of this abominable and shameful people.[7]

Next to them they employ the forces of the people for whom they are fighting, then auxiliary squadrons of their other allies, and finally they add a contingent of their own citizens, out of whom they appoint some man of tried valor to command the whole army. They add to him two substitutes, who hold no rank while he lives, but if he is taken

---

[7] Erasmus is plainly alluding to the Swiss when he says (*Adagia*, 482a), 'There is in Germany a nation, whose chief glory is to slay the greatest possible number. This is shocking in itself, but what makes it worse is that they do it for pay, like executioners paid for butchery.'

prisoner or killed, one of the two becomes as it were his heir and successor, and he, if it so happens, is succeeded by the third; thus they avoid the disorganization of the whole army through the death of the commander, the fortunes of war being always incalculable.

In each city a choice is made among those who volunteer; for no one is driven to fight abroad against his will, because they are convinced that if anyone is timorous by nature, he will not only not acquit himself manfully, but will make his companions cowardly. However, should any war assail their own country, they put the fainthearted, provided that they are physically fit, on shipboard among the braver sort, or put them here and there to man the walls, where they cannot run away: thus shame at being seen to flinch by their own side, the close quarters with the enemy, and the impossibility of escape combine to overpower their timidity, and often extreme danger makes them brave. Just as no one of the men is made to go against his will to a war outside the country, so if the wives are anxious to accompany their husbands to war,[8] not only do they not forbid it but even encourage them and incite them by commendation; when they have gone out, they are placed alongside of their husbands in battle, and each man is surrounded by his own children, relations and connections, so that those may be closest to each other and lend each other mutual assistance, whom nature most incites to help each other. It is the greatest reproach for a husband to return without his wife, or a wife without her husband, or for a son to come back having lost his father; so when it comes to hand-to-hand fighting, if the enemy stand their ground, the fight is long and melancholy, and ends with utter extermination. For as they take every care not to be

[8] Plato *Republic*, V. Tacitus *Germania*, XVIII.

obliged to fight themselves so long as they can finish the war by the hired assistance of substitutes, so when personal service is inevitable, they are most courageous in fighting, though they wisely avoided it as long as they might. They are not fierce in the first onslaught, but their strength increases by degrees through their stubborn resistance, for they would rather be cut to pieces than give way. For the absence of any anxiety about livelihood at home, and the removal of that worry which troubles us about the future of our families and everywhere breaks the highest spirit, makes a man hold his head high and disdain the foe. Moreover, their training in military discipline gives them confidence. Finally their good and sound opinions, in which they have been trained from boyhood, both by learning and by the good institutions of the state, give them additional courage. So they do not hold their lives so cheap as recklessly to throw them away, and not so immoderately dear, as shamefully to desire to keep them, when honor bids them lay them down. When the battle is everywhere most hot, a band of picked youths, who have taken an oath to devote themselves to the task, seek out the opposing general, and openly attack or secretly lie in ambush for him. Both from far and at close quarters he is assailed; a long and continued chain of men, fresh comers taking the place of those who are exhausted, keep up the attack; and it seldom happens, unless he look to his safety by running away, that he is not killed or does not fall alive into the enemy's hands. If the victory rests with them, there is no promiscuous carnage; for they would rather take the routed enemy prisoner than kill him; and they never pursue the flying enemy without keeping one division all the time drawn up ready for engagement. To such an extent is this the case that if, after the rest of the army has been beaten, they win the victory by this reserve force, they prefer to let the whole hostile force escape rather than get into the habit of pursuing the enemy in a disorderly way. They remember that more than once it has happened to themselves that, when the great bulk of their army has been beaten and routed, and the enemy flushed with their victory have been chasing the fugitives in all directions, a few of their number held in reserve, ready for emergencies, have suddenly attacked the scattered enemy, who feeling themselves quite safe were off their guard, have changed the whole fortune of the battle, and wresting out of the enemy's hand a certain and undoubted victory, have, though conquered, conquered their conquerors in turn. It is not easy to say whether they are more cunning in laying ambushes or more cautious in avoiding them. You would think they contemplated flight, when that is the very last thing that they intend: but on the other hand, when they do determine to flee, you would imagine they were thinking of anything but that. For if they feel themselves to be inferior in number or in position, either they noiselessly move away by night and pitch their camp elsewhere, or evade the enemy by some stratagem, or else by day they retire so imperceptibly and in such regular order, that it is as dangerous to attack them in retreat as it would be in advance. They protect their camps most carefully by a deep and broad ditch, the earth taken out of it being thrown inside; and they do not utilize the labor of ordinary workmen for the purpose, but the soldiers do it with their own hands, and the whole army is at work, except those who watch under arms in front of the rampart in case of emergencies. Thus through the efforts of so many they complete great fortifications, enclosing a large space with incredible speed.

They wear mail strong enough to turn blows but easily adapted to the motions and gestures of the body, so that they do not even feel any awkwardness in swimming in armor; for they practice swimming under arms as part of their apprenticeship in military discipline. The weapons they use at a distance are arrows, which they shoot with great strength and sureness of aim, not only on foot but also on horseback, while at close quarters they use not swords but axes, which deal a deadly blow with the point or with their weight, according as they cut or thrust with them. They are very clever in inventing engines of war, and when made they hide them with the greatest care lest, if made known before occasion requires them, they may be rather a laughingstock than serviceable. In making them, their first object is to have them easy to transport and handy to move round.

If a truce be made with the enemy, they keep it so religiously that they will not break it under any provocation. They do not ravage the enemy's country, nor burn his crops; nay, they will not even allow them to be trodden down by the feet of men or horses, as far as may he, thinking that they grow for their own benefit. They injure no non-combatant unless he be a spy. If cities be surrendered to them, they keep them intact. They do not even plunder those that they have stormed, but put to death the men who prevented a surrender, and make slaves of the rest of the defenders. They leave unharmed the noncombatants. If they find out that any recommended the surrender of the town, they give them a share of the property of those whom they have condemned, and the rest of the confiscated goods they present to their auxiliaries, for none of themselves touches the booty. When the war is over, they do not charge the friends, for whom they have borne the cost, with any part of it, but they put it down to the conquered, and under this head, make them not only pay money, which they lay aside for similar warlike purposes, but also surrender estates from which they may enjoy forever a large annual income. They now have such revenues in many countries, which being derived from various causes by degrees have grown to the sum of over seven hundred thousand ducats a year. To these estates they send some of their own citizens, under the title of Quaestor,[9] to live there in grand style and play the part of magnates. And yet there is much left over to put into the common treasury, unless they prefer to give the nation credit, which they often do until they require the use of the money, and even then it scarcely ever happens that they call in the whole sum. Out of these estates they confer a part on those who at their request undertake the dangerous mission, which I have previously described. If any king takes up arms against them and intends to invade their realm, they at once march out in great strength beyond their borders and meet him there; for they never lightly make war in their own country, nor is any emergency so pressing as to compel them to admit foreign auxiliaries into their island.

[9] The Quaestor was a Roman financial official. As the Roman Empire extended, each province was provided with one of them, who was subordinate to the Governor.

CHAPTER NINE

OF THE RELIGIONS IN UTOPIA[1]

There are different kinds of religion not only in various parts of the island, but also in each city. Some worship the Sun; others the Moon, others one of the planets as God. Some reverence a man who in former times was conspicuous for virtue or glory, not only as God, but as the supreme God. But the majority, and those the wiser among them, do nothing of the kind, but believe in one unknown Divine Power, eternal, incomprehensible, inexplicable, far beyond the reach of human intellect, diffused throughout the universe not in bulk but in power and potency. Him they call Father, to Him alone they attribute the beginnings, the growth, the progress, the changes and the ends of all things, and to no other do they give divine honors. Nay, all the others too, though varying in their belief, agree with them in this respect, that they think there is one supreme Being, to Whom we owe it that the whole world was made and is governed; and all alike call

[1] More is here describing the various forms of religion known to have existed in the world, and is chiefly drawing on Cicero *De Natura Deorum*, Book I, and Lactantius *De Falsa Religione*, Book I, 34.

Him in their native language, Mythra;[2] but in this respect they disagree, that He is looked on differently by different people, each thinking that whatever that be which he regards as supreme is that same nature, to Whose unique power and majesty the sum of all things by common consent is attributed. But gradually they are all beginning to depart from this medley of superstitions and are coming to agree together in that one religion which seems to surpass the rest in reasonableness. Nor is there any doubt that the other beliefs would have all disappeared long ago, had not anything untoward which chance brought upon men when they were thinking of changing their religion, been construed by fear as having not happened by chance but been sent from heaven, the Deity, Whose worship they were proposing to forsake, thus avenging an intention so impious toward Himself.

But when they heard from us the name of Christ, His teaching, His example, His miracles, and the no less wonderful constancy of the many martyrs, whose blood freely shed drew so many nations into their fellowship in many parts of the world, you cannot think how readily disposed they were to join it, whether through the secret inspiration of God, or because they thought it nearest to that belief which has the widest prevalence among them. But I think this, too, was of no small weight, that they heard from us that Christ approved the common way of living which they follow, and that it is still in use among the truest societies of Christians.[3] But whatever it was that influenced them, not a few agreed to adopt our religion and received holy baptism.

[2] Mithras, the Persian Sun-god, was widely worshipped in the Roman Empire. The language of Utopia was said to be 'like the Persian.'
[3] The marginal note refers this to monasteries, and is unquestionably right.

But as among us four (for that was all that was left, two of our company having died), there was, I am sorry to say, no priest, they were instructed in all other matters, but so far lack those sacraments, which with us only a priest can give; however, they understand what they are, and desire them with the greatest earnestness. Nay, they are even debating earnestly among themselves whether without the sending of a Christian bishop one chosen out of their own number may receive valid orders, and it seemed that they would choose one, but when I left, they had not yet done so. Even those who do not agree with the religion of Christ, do not try to deter others from it and do not oppose the instruction of any. One only of our company was interfered with, while I was there. He, as soon as he was baptized, in spite of our protests, began to speak publicly of Christ's religion with more zeal than discretion, and began to be so warm in his preaching, that not only did he prefer our worship to any other, but condemned all others as profane in themselves, and the followers of them impious and sacrilegious, and loudly declared they were worthy of eternal punishment. When he had long been preaching in this style, they arrested him, not for despising their religion, but for stirring up strife among the people, tried and convicted him, and sentenced him to exile. They count this among their most ancient institutions, that no one shall suffer for his religion. At the very beginning King Utopus—having heard that before his arrival the inhabitants had been continually quarrelling about religion, and having observed that the dissensions between the individual sects in fighting for their country had given him the opportunity of overcoming them all— after he had gained the victory, first ordained that it should be lawful for every man to follow what religion he chose; that each might strive to bring others over to his own,

provided that he quietly and peaceably supported his own
by reasoning and did not bitterly try to demolish that of
others; if his persuasions were not successful, he was to use
no violence and refrain from abuse, but if he contended too
vehemently in expressing his views, he was to be punished
by exile or enslavement.

Utopus ordained this not merely from regard to peace,
which he saw to be utterly destroyed by constant wrangling
and implacable hatred, but because he thought that this
peace was in the interest of religion itself. On religion he did
not venture to dogmatize himself, being doubtful whether
God did not inspire different people with different views,
and desire a varied and manifold worship. But assuredly he
thought it both insolence and folly to require by violence
and threats that all should agree with what you believe to
be true; moreover, if it should be the case that one religion is
true and all the rest false, he foresaw that if the matter were
dealt with reasonably and moderately, truth by its own natural force would come out and be clearly seen; but if there
were contention and armed violence were employed, seeing
that the worst men are always the most obstinate, the best
and holiest religion would be overwhelmed because of the
conflicting false religions, like corn overgrown by thorns
and bushes. So he left it all an open matter and made it free
to each to choose what he should believe, save that he strictly
gave injunction that no one should fall so far below the dignity of human nature as to believe that the soul perishes
with the body, or that the world is the mere sport of chance
and not governed by any divine providence.

This is why they believe that after this life vices are punished and virtue is rewarded; and if anyone thinks otherwise
they do not even regard him as a human being, seeing that
he has lowered the lofty nature of his soul to the level of the

brute beasts; so far are they from classing him among their citizens, whose laws and customs he would treat with contempt if it were not for fear. For who can doubt that he will strive either to evade by craft the common laws of his country, or to break them by violence, in order to serve his own private greed, when he has nothing to fear but the law, and no hope beyond the body? Wherefore one of this mind is excluded from office, is entrusted with no function, and is not put in charge of any public function; he is generally looked upon as of a mean and low disposition. But they do not punish him in any way, being convinced that it is in no man's power to believe whatever he chooses; nor do they compel him by threats to disguise his views, and they do not allow any deceptions or lies in the matter, for them they hate exceedingly as being next door to actual wrongdoing. They forbid him to argue in support of his opinion, at any rate before the common people, but in private before the priests and men of weight and importance they not only permit but encourage it, being sure that such madness will in the end give way to reason.

There are others too, and not so very few, who are not interfered with, because they are not bad men and there is something to be said for their view; these believe that animals have immortal souls, but not to be compared with ours in dignity and not destined to equal felicity. For almost all are absolutely certain that human bliss will be beyond measure; so that while they lament every man's diseases, they regret the death of no one but those whom they see depart from life in anxiety and unwillingly. For this they take to be a very bad omen, as though the soul, being without hope and having a guilty conscience, dreaded its departure through a secret premonition of impending punishment. Besides, they think that God will not be pleased with the coming of one who when summoned, does not gladly hasten to obey but is reluctantly drawn against his will. Thus those who behold this kind of death are filled with horror, and therefore carry him out to burial in melancholy silence, and then after praying to God to be merciful to his soul and graciously pardon his infirmities, they lay the corpse in the ground. But on the other hand, when men have died cheerfully and full of good hope, no one mourns for them, but they accompany the funeral with singing, with great affection commending their souls to God. Then with reverence rather than sorrow, they burn the bodies, and erect a pillar on the spot, on which the titles of the deceased are inscribed. On returning home they recount his character and his deeds, and no part of his life is more frequently or more gladly spoken of than his cheerful death.[4] They think that this memorial of virtue is not only the best means of stimulating the living to good deeds, but also the most acceptable form of attention to the dead, who are they think present when they are talked about, though invisible to the weak sight of mortals. For it would be inconsistent with the bliss of the departed not to be able to travel where they please, and it would be ungrateful of them absolutely to reject all desire of revisiting their friends, to whom they were bound in their lives by mutual love and affection, which like other good things they suppose to be increased after death rather than diminished in all good men. So they believe that the dead move about among the living, and are witnesses of their words and actions; and they therefore go about their business with more confidence relying on such protection, and the belief in the personal presence of their ancestors keeps men from all dishonest purposes. They utterly despise

---

[4] Roper's *Life of More* illustrates this in More's own case.

and deride auguries,[5] and all other divinations of false religion which are much accounted of in other countries. But miracles, which occur without the assistance of nature, they venerate as operations and witnesses of the Divine power at work; and such they say often occur there. Sometimes in great dangers they pray publicly for a sign, which they confidently look for and obtain. They think that to contemplate Nature and praise God in His works is a service acceptable to Him. There are some, and not so very few, who for religious motives eschew learning, and pursue no science, and do not devote themselves to leisure, but by various occupations and all good offices determine to win happiness after death. And so some tend the sick; others repair roads, clean out ditches, rebuild bridges, dig turf, sand and stone, fell and cut up trees, fetch wood, corn, and other things in carts into cities, and not only in the service of the public but of private persons render helpful, nay more than menial service. If anywhere there is a task so rough, hard and repulsive that most are deterred from it by the toil, disgust and despair involved, they gladly and cheerfully claim it all for themselves, and thus while perpetually engaged in hard work themselves, they secure leisure for others and yet claim no credit for it, and neither revile the life of others nor extol their own. The more such men put themselves in the position of servants, the more are they honored by all.[6]

They have two sects, whose opinions and practice differ accordingly. One is that of those who live single, and not only

---

[5] The Roman soothsayer (augur) was chiefly occupied with the flight of birds, but also derived omens from the feeding of sacred fowls, lightning, dreams, and all mysterious occurrences.

[6] More need not have been thinking of the Frati della Misericordia of Florence, for all English guilds had a charitable side to their activities.

eschew all carnal intercourse but abstain from flesh-meat and in some cases from all animal food. They entirely reject the pleasures of this life as harmful, and are merely set upon the hope of the life to come, hoping to obtain it shortly by watchings and labors, and in the meantime they are cheerful and sprightly. The other is just as fond of hard labor, but regards matrimony as preferable to the single state, not despising the comfort which it brings, and thinking that their duty to nature requires them to work, and their duty to their country to beget children. They avoid no pleasure, unless it interferes with their labor. They like flesh-meat just because they think that this fare makes them stronger for any work. The Utopians regard these as the wiser, but the first named as the holier men. If the latter based on reason their preference of celibacy to matrimony and of a hard life to an easy one, they would laugh them to scorn; but as they say they are prompted by religion, they look up to and reverence them. For there is nothing they are more careful about than not lightly to dogmatize on any point of religion. Such then are these whom in their own language they call by a name of their own, Buthrescae, which may be translated 'men of religion.'[7]

They have priests of great holiness, and therefore very few; for they have not more than thirteen in each city, with a like number of churches. But when they go to war, seven go with the army, and the same number of substitutes is appointed till they come back and return to their former duties; then those who are above the number, until the others die and they succeed to their places, in the meantime attend upon the Bishop, who is the head of all. They are elected by the people just like the other magistrates, by secret

[7] This coinage in Greek would mean 'exceedingly religious.' The Latin equivalent More gives is 'religiosus.'

ballot, to avoid canvassing, and when elected are ordained by their college. They preside over worship, and order religious ceremonies, and are censors of morals, and it is counted a great disgrace for a man to be summoned before them, or reproved as being of reprobate life. It is their part to give advice and admonition; but to correct and punish offenders belongs to the Prince and the other magistrates, though the priests excommunicate those whom they find to be evil-livers, and there is no punishment which is more dreaded. For they incur very great disgrace and are tortured by a secret religious fear, and even their bodies will not long go scot free; for if they do not demonstrate to the satisfaction of the priests their speedy repentance, they are arrested and punished by the Council for impiety. To the priests is entrusted the education of childhood and youth, and they regard the care of their morals and behavior as equally important with their advancement in learning for they take the greatest pains from the very first to instill into the minds of children, while they are still tender and pliable, good opinions which are useful for the preservation of their commonwealth; for these, when they are firmly implanted in children, will accompany them when grown up all through their lives, and are of great benefit toward maintaining the state of a commonwealth, which never decays except through vices which arise out of wrong opinions.

The priests, unless they be women (for women are not debarred from the priesthood, but only seldom chosen and none but widows and elderly women), have for their wives the chosen women of the country. For to no other office in Utopia is so much honor given, so much so that even if they have committed any crime, they are not subjected to any public tribunal, but left to God and to themselves: for they think it wrong to lay human hands on one, however guilty,

who has been consecrated to God in so special a manner as a
holy offering. It is easier for them to observe this custom,
because their priests are so few and so carefully chosen. For
it very seldom happens that one who is elevated to such dignity as being the most virtuous among the good, nothing but
virtue being taken into account, falls into corruption and
wickedness; and if he does so fall, human nature being ever
prone to change, yet since they are but few and are invested
with no power but only raised to honor, it need not be feared
that it will cause ruin to the commonwealth. Indeed they
have but few priests, to prevent the dignity of the order,
which they now reverence so highly, being lowered and
cheapened by the honor being given broadcast, especially as
they think it hard to find many so good that they are fit for
so honorable a position, for the filling of which it is not
enough to be endowed with ordinary virtues. They are
not more esteemed among their own people than in foreign
countries, which can easily be seen from a fact, which is, I
think, its cause. When the armies are fighting in battle, they
are to be found separate but not far off, kneeling, dressed in
their sacred vestments, with hands upstretched to heaven,
and praying first of all for peace, next for victory to their own
side, but without bloodshed to either side. When their side is
winning, they run among the combatants and restrain the
fury of their own men against the routed enemy. Merely to
see and appeal to them suffices to save the lives of the enemy:
and to touch their flowing garments protects the suppli-
ant's goods from spoliation. This has brought them such
veneration among all nations, and given them so real a majesty, that they have saved their own citizens from the enemy
as often as they have protected the enemy from their own
men. It is well known that sometimes when their own side
has given way, when the case was desperate and they were

taking to flight, and the enemy were rushing on to plunder and to kill, the carnage has been averted by the intervention of the priests, and when the armies have been parted from one another, peace has been concluded and settled on equal terms. For never was there any nation so savage, cruel and barbarous, that it has not regarded their bodies as sacred and inviolable.

They keep as holy days the first and the last of each month, and also the first and last days of the year, which they divide into months; and these they measure by the orbit of the moon just as they reckon the year by the course of the sun. In their language they call the first days Cynemernes, and the last days Trapemernes, which names have the same meaning as if they were rendered First Feasts and Last Feasts.[8]

Their churches are fine sights, being not only elaborate in workmanship, but also capable of holding a vast congregation, which is necessary, there being so few of them. But they are all rather dark, which is not due to the ignorance of the builders, but to the deliberate intention of the priests, because they think that abundant light makes the thoughts wander, while scantier and subdued light concentrates the mind and is conducive to more earnest devotion.[9] And since the religion of all is not the same, and yet all its fashions, though varied and manifold, by different roads as it were, all tend to the same end, the worship of the Divine Nature; therefore nothing is seen or heard in the churches which does not seem

[8] Cynemerne κυνὸς ἡμέρα, literally the dog's day of the month. Trapemerne τρέπειν ἡμέρα, literally the turning day of the month.

[9] Milton *Il Penseroso* 159 'Storied windows richly dight, Casting a dim religious light.' Mr. Lupton quotes Pope *Eloisa to Abelard*, 'Where awful arches make a noonday night, and the dim windows shed a solemn light.'

to agree with the common belief. If any sect has a rite of its own, it is performed within the walls of each man's house. Therefore no image of God is seen in a church, so that it may be free for each to conceive of God according to his own belief in any similitude he pleases. They have no special name for God except that of Mythra, by which word they agree to represent the one nature of the Divine Majesty whatever it be; and the prayers formulated are such as every man may utter without offense to his own sect. They come, therefore, to the church in the evening of the last days of the month and year, still fasting, to thank God for the prosperity they have enjoyed in the year or month, of which it is the last day; then next day, which is the first feast, they assemble at the churches in the morning to pray for good luck and prosperity in the ensuing year or month, of which this feast is the beginning. At the last feasts the wives, before they go to church, fall down at the feet of their husbands, and the children before their parents, and confess that they have offended, either by losing something or carelessly performing some duty, and pray for pardon for their offense. So if any cloud of quarrel in the family has arisen, it is dispelled by this satisfaction, so that with clear and pure minds they may be present at divine service; for religion forbids them to be present with troubled conscience. So if they are conscious of hatred or anger against anyone, they do not come to service until they are reconciled and have cleansed their hearts, for fear of swift and condign punishment. When they reach the church they part, the men going to the right side, and the women to the left. Then they arrange their places so that the males in each house sit in front of the head of the family, and the mother of the family is behind the womenfolk. Thus they take care that every gesture abroad is observed by those by whose authority and discipline they are governed at home.

They also carefully see to it that everywhere the younger are placed in the company of the elder, lest if children be put with children they may spend in childish folly the time in which they ought most to he conceiving a religious fear of God, the greatest and almost the only stimulus to good living. They slay no beast in sacrifice, and cannot believe that the Divine Mercy delights in bloodshed and slaughter, seeing that it has given life to animals that they might live and not die. They burn incense and other sweet savors, and also offer a great number of candles, not that they are unaware that these things add nothing to the divine nature, any more than do the prayers of men, but they like this harmless kind of worship, and feel somehow that by these perfumes and lights and other ceremonies they are uplifted and raised with livelier devotion to the worship of God. The people wear white clothes in church, the priest wears vestments of various colors, of wonderful design, but not as costly material as one would expect; for they are not interwoven with gold or set with precious stones, but wrought with the different feathers of birds so cleverly and skillfully that no costly material could have equaled the value of the design. Moreover, in these birds' wings and feathers, and the fixed orders by which they are distinguished in the priest's vestment, they say certain hidden mysteries are contained, by knowing the meaning of which, as it is carefully handed down by the priests, they are reminded of the loving kindness of God to them, and in turn of their own piety toward God and duty toward one another.[10]

---

[10] Plato *Timaeus* 91D, 'Innocent light-minded men who thought to study the heavens by sight, were changed into birds and grew feathers instead of hair.' This passage may have suggested to More the garb of the priests in Utopia.

When the priest thus arrayed first comes out of the inner sanctuary, all forthwith fall on the ground in reverence with such deep silence all round, that the very sight fills them with holy awe, and they feel that God is really present. After remaining awhile on the ground, at a signal from the priest they rise; then they sing praises to God, which they diversify with musical instruments often, of different shapes from those which are seen in our part of the world. Many of them surpass in sweetness those in use with us, but some are not comparable with ours. But in one thing undoubtedly they are far ahead of us, that all their music, whether played on instruments, or sung by the human voice, so renders and expresses the natural feelings, the sound being suited to the matter (whether it be prayer, or an expression of joy, placability, trouble, mourning, or anger, and so represents the meaning by the fashion of the melody), that it wonderfully affects, penetrates and influences the minds of the hearers. At last the priest and people together repeat solemn forms of prayer, so drawn up, that every man may apply to himself what all request together. In these every man recognizes God to be the Author of his creation, direction, and all other blessings, and thanks Him for all the benefits he has received; particularly that by the favor of God he has come into a commonwealth which is most happy, and obtained a religion which he hopes to be most true. If in this he be in error, or if there is anything better than either, of which God approves more, he prays that He will, of His goodness, bring him to the knowledge of it, for he is ready to follow in whatever direction he may be led; but if this constitution be the best and his religion the most true, then that He may give him steadfastness in the same and bring all other men to the same way of living and the same opinion of God, unless there be anything in this variety of religions which is according to His inscrutable will. Finally he prays that He would take him to Himself by an easy death, how soon or late, he does not venture to determine, though if it might be without offense to His Majesty, it would be much more welcome to him to die a very hard death and go to God than to be kept long away from Him by a prosperous career in life. After this prayer has been said, they fall down on the ground again, then after an interval rise and go away to dinner, and the rest of the day they pass in games and the exercises of military training.

Now I have described to you, as truly as I could, the constitution of that commonwealth, which I think not only the best but the only one which can rightly claim the name of a commonwealth. For in all others men talk freely of the public good, but only look after their own. Here, where there is no private property, they seriously mind the affairs of state. Assuredly in both cases there is good reason. For elsewhere there are few who do not understand that unless they make some separate provision for themselves, however much the commonwealth may flourish, they will themselves starve; so necessity compels them to think that they must take account of themselves rather than the people, that is, of others than themselves. On the other hand, here, where all things are common, no one doubts that the individual will always have plenty, provided the common granaries are well filled. For the distribution of good things is not niggardly; and there are no poor, and no beggars: though no man has anything, yet all are rich. For what can be greater riches for a man than to live in joy and peace, with no anxieties as to the future, not troubled about food, nor harassed by the querulous demands of his wife, not fearing poverty for his son, not worrying about his daughter's dowry, and without anxiety about his own livelihood or that of his belongings, his wife, sons, grandsons, great-grandsons, great-great-grandsons and all the long succession of descendants that gentlefolk anticipate, but sure of their happiness? Then take into account the fact that there is no less provision for those who have been laborers but are now past work, than for those who are still laboring. Here I should like anyone to be so bold as to compare this fair system with the so-called justice practiced in other nations, among whom, upon my word, I cannot discover any trace of justice and fairness. For what justice is it that a noble, or a goldsmith, or a moneylender, or in fact any other of the idle classes, whose work, if they do any, is not very essential to the commonwealth, should live in grandeur and luxury, doing nothing at all or only that which is superfluous? But in the meantime, the day laborer, the carter, the smith, the husbandman, by continuous toil, that beasts of burden could scarcely endure, and toil so essential, that no state could last for a year without it, get such a poor living, and lead such a miserable life, that the condition of beasts of burden might seem far preferable; for these have not to work so incessantly, they are not much worse fed, and they get more enjoyment out of it, and have no fear for the future. The laborers not only have to work without return or profit at the time, but are agonized by the thought of a helpless and indigent old age; for their daily wage is too scanty to suffice even for the day, much less can they spare or save anything that can be laid by for their needs when they are old.

Now is not this an unjust and ungrateful commonwealth, which lavishes such great rewards on gentle folk, as they call them, and goldsmiths and such other persons, who are either idle, or mere parasites and purveyors of empty pleasures, but has no kind care for husbandmen, colliers, day laborers, carters and smiths, without whom there would be no commonwealth at all? But after it has misused their labor in their prime, then, when they are weighed down with age and disease, and in utter want, it forgets all the benefits it has received at their hands, and ungratefully requites them with a most miserable death. And what is worse, the rich every day take away a part of the daily allowance of the poor not only by private fraud but by statute law, and thus they have now made worse what even before seemed unjust, that those who have deserved best of the commonwealth should have the worst return for their labors; and yet by the statutes they have passed, this becomes justice. So when I consider and turn over in my mind the state of all flourishing common-wealths today, so help me God, I can see nothing but a conspiracy of the rich, who are aiming at their own advan-tage under the name and title of the commonwealth. They invent and devise all ways and means, by which they may keep without fear of losing all that they have amassed by evil practices, and next to that may purchase as cheaply as possible, and misuse the labor and toil of the poor.

These devices forthwith become law, when the rich have once decreed in the name of the state, that is of the poor as well as the rich, that they should be observed. But when these evil men by insatiable greed have divided up among themselves what would have been enough for all, yet how far are they from the felicity of Utopia? When in Utopia all greed for money was entirely removed with its use, what a mass of troubles was lopped off, how great a crop of crimes was pulled up by the roots! For who does not know that fraud, theft, rapine, quarrels, disorders, strife, seditions, murders, treasons, poisonings, which are punished rather than restrained by daily executions, die out with the death of money, and that fear, anxiety, worries, toils and watch-ings will perish along with money? Poverty itself, which seemed only to lack money, would forthwith disappear and die out if money were removed. To make this more clear, consider in your thoughts some barren and unfruitful year, in which many thousands of men have been carried off by hunger. I am sure that at the end of that scarcity, if the rich man's granaries had been searched, so much corn might have been found as, if it had been divided among those who were killed off by hunger and disease, would have prevented anyone from feeling that meagre return of climate and soil. So easily might men get their living, if that much-lauded money, that grand invention to open the way to a living, did not exist and form the only barrier in the way of our getting a living. I doubt not that even the rich perceive that it would be a much better state of things to lack no necessity than to have abundance of superfluities, to be released from such numerous troubles than to be hemmed in by great riches. Nor do I doubt that regard for a man's own advantage, or the authority of our Savior Christ—Who, of His wisdom, could not fail to know what was best, and of His goodness could not advise what He knew not to be best— would long ago have brought the world to adopt the laws of this commonwealth, had not one single monster, the chief and progenitor of all plagues, Pride, stood in the way. She measures prosperity not by her own good, but by the harm of others. She would not even consent to be made a goddess, if no poor wretches were left for her to domineer over, over whose miseries her good fortune might shine in comparison, whose poverty she might vex and torment by unfolding her own wealth. This serpent of Hell enters the hearts of men and stops them from entering on the better path of life, and is so deeply rooted in men that she cannot easily be plucked out. That this constitution, which I should be glad to see all enjoy, has been the good fortune of the Utopians, fills me with rejoicing. They have adopted such institutions of

life as have laid the foundations of a commonwealth not
only most happily, but also to last forever, so far as human
prescience can forecast. For when at home, along with other
vices, ambition and factiousness have been uprooted, there
is no danger of trouble from domestic discord, which has
been the only cause of ruin to the well-established prosperity of many cities.

But while harmony is preserved at home and its institutions are in a healthy state, not all the envy of the neighboring
kings, though it has often attempted it and been repelled,
can avail to shake or even to influence that realm.

When Raphael had finished his story, many things came
to my mind which seemed very absurd in the manners and
laws of that people, not only in their way of waging wars,
their ceremonies, their religion, and their other institutions,
but most of all in that which is the chief foundation of their
whole structure, the community of life and goods without
any money dealings. For by this alone all the nobility, mag-
nificence, splendor and majesty, the true glories and
ornaments of a commonwealth are utterly overthrown. Yet
since I knew he was wearied with his tale and I was not certain that he could brook any opposition to his views,
particularly as I remember that he had censured others on
account of their fear that they might not seem to be wise
enough, unless they found some fault with other men's
inventions, therefore I praised their way of life, and his
speech, and took him by the hand and led him in to supper,
first saying that we would have another opportunity of
thinking more deeply on these topics and discussing them
with him more fully: and I wish this might some day come
to pass. Meanwhile, though in other ways he is a man of
most undoubted learning and of great knowledge of the
world, yet I cannot agree with all that he said; but I readily

admit that there are many things in the Utopian common-wealth, which it is easier to wish for in our own states than to have any hope of seeing realized.

THE END.

———————

A stanza on the Island Utopia, by Anemolius, Poet Laureate, Sister's son to Hythlodaye:—

> Utopia, hight of old, as thing of fancy,
> Rival I am of Plato's commonwealth,
> Perchance its vanquisher (for what in words
> She shadowed forth, alone I realized
> In men, in wealth, and in laws excellent),
> Eutopia now deserve I to be called.

LETTERS

THOMAS MORE TO PETER GILLES, GREETING (I)

I am almost ashamed, well-beloved Peter Gilles, to send you this book about the commonwealth of Utopia after almost a year, when I am sure you looked for it within a month and a half. For you know that I was relieved of all the labor of invention in the work and had not to think at all about the arrangement of the subject, but only to repeat, what in your company I heard Raphael relate. So there was no reason for me to take trouble about the language of the narrative, seeing that his conversation could not be expressed with elaboration, being as it was, extemporary and without premeditation, and that of one who, as you know, was not so well acquainted with Latin as with Greek; therefore the nearer my style came to his plain and straightforward speech, the nearer it would be to the truth, for which alone I care and which alone I am bound to care for. I confess, my dear Peter, that all this being at my disposal, I was relieved of so much trouble, that scarcely anything remained for me to do. Otherwise the invention or arrangement of the subject might have required both some time and study of a talent neither contemptible nor quite unlearned. Now if it had been required, that the matter should be written down, not only truly but eloquently, I could not have performed the task by any time or study. But as it is, these cares being removed, on which I should have had to work so hard, and since it only remained for me to write out simply what I heard, there was no difficulty about it. But even to carry through this simple task, my other tasks left me practically no leisure at all. While I am constantly engaged in legal business, either pleading or hearing, or giving an award in arbitration, or deciding a matter as judge, while I am paying a friendly visit to one man or going on business to another, while I devote almost the whole day to other men's affairs, and what remains of it, to my family at home, I leave to myself, that is to writing, nothing at all.

For when I have returned home, I must converse with my wife, chat with my children, and talk to my servants. All this I count as business, for it has got to be done—and it is quite necessary unless you want to be a stranger in your own home—and one must take care to be as agreeable as possible to those whom nature has provided, or chance made, or you yourself have chosen to be companions of your life, provided you do not spoil them by kindness or through indulgence make them your masters instead of your servants. In these occupations that I have named, the day, the month, the year slip away. When then can we find time to write? Nor have I yet said anything about sleep, nor even of meals, which for many take up as much time as sleep, and that takes up almost half a man's life. So I only get for myself the time I can filch from sleep and food. Slowly, therefore, because this is but little, yet at last, as it is something, I have finished *Utopia*, and sent it to you, dear Peter, to read and remind me of anything that has escaped me. For though in this respect I do not entirely distrust myself (I only wish I were as good in wit and learning as I am not altogether deficient in memory), yet I am not so confident as to believe that I have forgotten nothing. For John Clement, my pupil,[1] who, as you know, was present at this conversation, as indeed I like him to hear any conversation of profit (for from this young plant, which has begun to put forth shoots in Greek and Latin literature, I expect no small increase some day), caused me to feel very doubtful on one point. Hythlodaye, according to my recollection declared that the bridge which spans the river Anyder at Amaurote is five hundred paces in length: but my John says that two hundred must be taken off, for the river is not more than three hundred paces in breadth. Please recall the matter to mind. For if you agree with him, I shall adopt your view and think myself mistaken; but if you do not remember, I shall put down, as I have done, what I think I remember; for as I have taken great pains that there shall be nothing false in the book, so if there is doubt about anything, I shall rather be inaccurate by mistake than intentionally deceive; for I would rather be honest than wise. But it will be easy for you to remedy this defect, if you ask Raphael himself by word of mouth or by letter, if he has gone away: which you needs must do on account of another difficulty which has cropped up, whether through my fault or yours or Raphael's. For I forgot to ask, and he forgot to say, in what part of the new world Utopia lies. I would give a large sum rather than that this should be omitted, partly because I am rather ashamed to be ignorant, in what sea lies the island of which I am saying so much, partly because there are several among us and one in particular, a good

---

[1] Clemens, qui literis et Latinis et Græcis ita proficit indies ut non exiguam de eo spem concipiam futurum eum aliquando et patriaæ et literis ornamento.'—More to Erasmus, 17 February (?) 1516.

man and a doctor of divinity,[2] who is exceedingly anxious to visit Utopia, not from the idle curiosity of investigating novelties, but to promote and spread our religion, the seeds of which have been so successfully sown. That he may duly perform this, he has made up his mind to seek a mission from the Pope, and even to ask that he may be made Bishop of Utopia, being in no wise deterred by any scruple that he must sue for this Bishopric; for he thinks that a holy suit, which proceeds from a pious zeal, and not from any consideration of honor or gain. Therefore I beg you, Peter, either by word of mouth if you conveniently can, or by letter, to address Hythlodaye and see that there be nothing included in my work which is false, or wanting to it which is true. Perhaps it will be best for the book to be shown to him. For no one else is so well able to correct its mistakes, nor can he do this at all, unless he reads what I have written. Moreover, in this way you will find out whether he hears with pleasure, or is annoyed, that this work is written by me. For if he has determined to put down in writing his own adventures, perhaps he may not want me to do so; and I should certainly not like to forestall him and rob his narrative of the flower and grace of novelty, by making known the commonwealth of Utopia. Yet, to tell the truth, I have not yet made up my mind myself, whether I shall publish it at all. For so various are the tastes of men, so wayward the characters of some, so ungrateful their minds, so wrong-headed their judgments, that those are much better off, who follow their own bent in pleasure and enjoyment, than those who worry themselves with

---

[2] According to a note in Robynson's translation (1624 edition) this was Rowland Phillips, formerly Fellow of Oriel and Warden of Merton, Vicar of Croydon and Canon of St. Paul's. He is mentioned in the letters written by More from prison, as taking the oath to the Act of Supremacy.

anxiety to publish something that may bring profit or pleasure to others, who yet receive it with disdain or ingratitude. Most men are devoid of learning; many despise it. The barbarous reject as hard whatever is not positively barbarous. The smatterer despises as commonplace, whatever is not packed with obsolete expressions. Some people only approve of what is old, some only admire their own work. One is so grim that he will not hear of a joke; another is so stupid that he cannot endure wit. Some are so blunt of perception that they fear sarcasm as much as one bitten by a mad dog fears water. Some are so changeable that they praise one thing sitting and another thing standing. These sit in taverns, and over their cups criticize the talents of authors, and with great superiority condemn each, as they please, according to his writings, plucking each as it were by the hair, while remaining under cover, and as the proverb goes, out of shot, being themselves so smooth and shorn, that they present not even a hair of an honest man by which they may be caught hold of. Besides, others are so ungrateful, that though extremely delighted with the work, they do not any the more love the author; not unlike discourteous guests, who when they have been profusely entertained at a rich banquet, go home well filled, without thanking him who invited them. Go now, and cater at your own expense for men of such dainty palate, such varied taste, and of such forgetful and thankless natures! But, nevertheless, do as I said with Hythlodaye. Afterward it will be open to me to take fresh counsel on the subject. However, if it be with his consent (since after I have gone through the labor of writing, it is too late for me to be wise now) in the matter of publication that remains, I will follow the advice of my friends, and yours first and foremost. Farewell, my dear friend, with your excellent wife; and love me as you have ever done, for I love you even more than I ever did.

TO THE MOST ILLUSTRIOUS
JEROME BUSLEIDEN,

PROVOST OF AIRE AND COUNCILOR TO THE CATHOLIC KING CHARLES, PETER GILLES OF ANTWERP SENDS GREETING

The other day, most eminent Busleiden, Thomas More, whom you know well, and can testify, as I do, that he is the greatest ornament of our age, sent me his book of the Island Utopia, known to few as yet, but eminently worthy to he made known to all, as being far superior to Plato's *Republic.* This is now set forth, described and brought vividly before our eyes by a man of great eloquence in such a way that, when I read it, I think I see far more than when, being present along with More at the conversation, I heard Raphael Hythlodaye's own words. And yet Hythlodaye, a man of no ordinary power of expression, so set forth his subject, that it could easily be seen that he was not repeating what he had heard from the accounts of others, but telling things that he had seen with his own eyes and of which he had had long personal experience; and he is a man to my mind superior to Ulysses himself in his knowledge of countries, men and things, such as I think has no equal anywhere in the last eight hundred years, and in comparison of whom Vespucci himself may be thought to have seen nothing. Apart from the fact that all tell more effectively what they have seen than what they have heard, the man had a skill of his own in unfolding his narrative. But when I look on the same picture as painted by More's brush, I feel sometimes as if I were actually living in Utopia. I am even disposed to think that in all the five years which Raphael spent in the island, he did not see so much as may be perceived in More's description. There is such a quantity of marvelous things, that I am at a loss, which I am to admire most, the successfulness of a faithful memory, which could repeat almost word for word matters which he had just heard, or the sagacity with which he notes all the sources from which either evils actually arise to the commonwealth or blessings might arise, all quite unknown to ordinary folk, or the force and fluency of his language, which in pure Latin style and strong nervous expressions has embraced so many matters. And yet few are more distracted than he in attending to both private and public business. But this will not so much surprise you, most learned Busleiden, for you know him intimately as a man of superhuman and almost divine intellect. For the rest there is nothing I can add to what he has written. But there was a verse of four lines in the Utopian native tongue which, after More's departure, Hythlodaye happened to show me, and this I have caused to be added to the book, with the alphabet used by the people, and have added some few notes in the margin.

As to More's difficulty about the geographical position of the island, Raphael did not fail to mention it, but in very few words, and by the way, as if reserving the subject for another occasion. But, somehow or other, we both failed to catch what he said, owing to an unlucky accident. While Raphael was speaking, one of More's servants had come up to him to whisper something to him, and so his attention was diverted. I was therefore listening all the more intently, when one of the company, who had, I suppose, caught cold on shipboard, coughed so loudly that I lost something of what Raphael said. However, I shall not rest till I have got full information on this point, so that I shall be able to tell you exactly not only the longitude but also the latitude of the island, provided that our friend Hythlodaye be alive. For there are various reports about him. Some say that he died on his journey home. Others say that on his return to his native land, partly because he could not endure their ways and partly because he missed Utopia so much, he made his way back again to that country.

As to the difficulty that the name of this island is not to be found in old descriptions of the world, that was well explained by Hythlodaye himself: it was possible, he said, either that the name used by the ancients had afterwards been changed, or that this island escaped their notice, just as nowadays we find many countries cropping up, which were unknown to the ancient geographers. But what is the use of finding arguments to make the account more credible, when we have More to vouch for it? That he is doubtful about publication, makes me praise and acknowledge his modesty. But from every point of view I thought it unfair to suppress the work and most fit that it should go out to the world, especially with the recommendation of your name, not only because you are specially acquainted with More's talents, but also because no man is better fitted than you to assist with good counsels the commonwealth, in which you have labored for many years, winning great praise for wisdom and integrity. Farewell, kind patron of learned pursuits and ornament of our age.

ANTWERP. Nov. 1st, 1516.

JEROME BUSLEIDEN TO THOMAS MORE, GREETING

It was not enough for you, most distinguished More, to have long devoted all your pains, labor and energy to the interest and advantage of individuals; but your kindness and generosity have prompted you to bestow them to the general good; for you thought that this benefit of yours, whatever it might be, deserved the greater popularity, aimed at the higher favor and sought the greater glory, in proportion as it was likely to profit the greater number, when more widely extended and conferred on more recipients. Though you have always aimed at this on other occasions, yet you have recently secured your object with wonderful success, by putting down in writing that afternoon conversation, by which you have given to the world a description of the perfect constitution, which all must desire, in the Utopian commonwealth. In your happy description of that fair system we cannot miss anything either of consummate learning or complete knowledge of the world in which we live; for both meet so perfectly on an equality, that neither confesses itself beaten, but both contend on equal terms for the palm of glory.

For you are so well equipped with varied learning and with wide and unerring knowledge of the world, that what you write, you state on the grounds of experience, while you write with the greatest cleverness what you have determined to state. Truly a wonderful and most uncommon felicity, which is the rarer, as it jealously withholds itself from most, and is only given to few, chiefly to those who, as they have the candor to wish, so have the learning, credit and authority which enables them to serve the common good as faithfully, honestly and wisely, as you do now; for regarding yourself as "born not for yourself alone, but for the whole world," you have thought it worth while by your fair merit to lay the whole world under an obligation.

In no other way could you have secured this object better or more rightly than by holding up before reasonable mortals that ideal of a commonwealth, that pattern and finished model of morality, than which none has ever been seen in the world more sound in its institution or more perfect or more desirable; for it is far superior and leaves far behind the much lauded polities of Sparta, Athens and Rome. If they had been founded under the same auspices and regulated by the same institutions, laws, decrees, and morals as this commonwealth of yours, assuredly they would not even now have been ruined and leveled to the ground, and now, alas, prostrated without any hope of recovery; nay, they would still be intact, prosperous, flourishing and happy, mistresses of the world, and sharing their wide dominion by land and sea. You pitied the unhappy fate of these commonwealths, and you wished to save the states which today wield imperial sway from a like vicissitude of fortune, by your ideal state, which devoted its energies not so much to forming laws as to training the most approved magistrates (and not without reason, for otherwise, if we agree with Plato, the best laws would be counted dead), because after their likeness, the pattern of their virtue, the example of their conduct, the picture of their justice, the whole state and right course of any perfect commonwealth should be modeled, so that, above all else, there is a combination of wisdom in the ruling classes, bravery in the soldiers, temperance in individuals, and justice in all.

Since the commonwealth, which you make so famous, is obviously a happy blend of all these qualities, no wonder, if on this account it comes to be not only formidable to many, but revered by the whole world and worthy to be celebrated by all generations to come; and the more so because in it all wrangling about possession is excluded and no one has any property of his own; but with a view to the common interest all men have all things in common, so that every matter and every action, however small, whether public or private, regards not the greed of the many or the caprice of the few, but is entirely directed to the maintenance of one uniform justice, equality and fellowship. When that is its single aim, there must be an entire removal of all that feeds, enflames and lights intrigues, luxury, jealousy and oppression, into which mortals are sometimes driven, even though reluctant, by the holding of private property, or the fierce desire of gain or that most pitiable of passions, ambition, to their own great and unparalleled loss. For from these causes often arise suddenly disagreements, military preparations, and wars worse than civil, by which not only is the prosperous state of flourishing commonwealths completely destroyed, but their old renown, their past triumphs, glorious trophies, and rich spoils so often won by the conquest of enemies, are completely wiped out.

If in these points my testimony should win less credit than I could wish, there will be to hand the most reliable witnesses I can refer you to, in all the great cities laid waste of old, the states destroyed, the commonwealths overthrown, the villages burnt and consumed, of which there are now scarce any traces or relics to be seen of their great ruin, and hardly are their names recorded by any history, however old and far-reaching. Such notable disasters, devastations, overthrows and calamities of war, our states one and all will easily escape, provided that they organize themselves exactly on the pattern of the Utopian commonwealth, and do not depart from it by a hair's breadth. By so doing, and only so, will they recognize in the end most fully how greatly they have benefited by the service you have rendered them, especially because thereby they will have learned how to preserve their own state safe, unharmed and triumphant: accordingly their debt to you, their savior in the hour of need, will be that which is justly due to one who not only preserves an individual citizen, but a whole state.

Meanwhile farewell, and continue to devise, execute and perfect ever fresh benefits to your country, which will make it eternal and yourself immortal. Farewell, most learned and most philanthropic More, glory of your Britain, and of this world of ours.

From my house at Mechlin, 1516.

JEROME BUSLEIDEN TO HIS FRIEND ERASMUS, GREETING

Here at length is the letter for you which you told me to compose. In it if I have performed less than your expectations of me or the dignity of the subject required, you must look to it yourself, and blame no one else, that you committed the task to one so ill able to express himself, and generally unfit. It is enough for him at least to have attempted, what he was not able to perform; and he hopes that the trouble he has taken in the matter does not altogether meet with your disapproval, especially as in doing it he complied with your wishes, at some risk to his credit and loss of his reputation. It is certainly a most clear and indubitable proof of my regard for you, and as such, I trust you will do your best for it, and this will most assuredly be the case if you think fit to polish with the file of your pure and correct style my rusty and uncouth letter. Meanwhile farewell, and remember me to the eminent ambassador[1] of His Majesty the King of England.

In haste.

MECHLIN. 9th Nov. 1516.

---

[1] Cuthbert Tunstall.

THOMAS MORE TO PETER GILLES, GREETING (II)

I was extremely pleased with the criticism of my work, with which you are acquainted, by a clever person, who put this dilemma about Utopia. 'If the facts as reported are true, I see some absurdities in them; but if fictitious, I find More's finished judgment in some respects wanting.' Whoever he was, I am much obliged to him, Peter; I suspect him to be learned, and I can see he is friendly. By this frank criticism he has obliged me more than anyone else since the appearance of the book. For in the first place, attracted by interest in me or the work, he seems not to have wearied of the labor, but read it all through, not perfunctorily and hastily, as priests go through the Hours, but so slowly and carefully as to pay attention to details. Secondly, by objecting to some things, he has given a tacit approval to the rest. Finally, in the very words in which he censures me, he gives me more praise than all who have praised me of set purpose. For he shows that he thinks highly of me, when he complains of disappointment when he reads something not finished, since it would be more than I could hope if I did not write some things that are absurd among so many. Yet if I may in my turn deal faithfully with him, I do not see why so sharp-eyed a critic, because he has detected some absurdities in the institutions of Utopia, or I have devised some things inexpedient in the framing of a constitution, should be so minded as if there were nothing absurd in the world, or as if any philosopher had ever ordered the state, or even his own house, without instituting something that had better be changed. Why, if the memory of great men were not hallowed by time, I could in each of them quote points, in the condemnation of which I should get a unanimous vote. Now, when he doubts whether Utopia is real or fictitious, I find his finished judgment wanting. I do not pretend that if I had determined to write about the commonwealth and had remembered such a story, I should have shrunk from a fiction, by which the truth, as if smeared with honey, might more pleasantly flow into men's minds. But if I wanted to abuse the ignorance of common folk, I should certainly have been careful to prefix some indications for the learned to see through my purpose. Thus if I had put nothing but the names of prince, river, city and island such as might suggest to the learned that the island was nowhere, the city a phantom, the river without water, and the prince without a people, this would not have been hard to do, and would have been much wittier than what I did; for if the faithfulness of an historian had not been binding on me, I am not so stupid as to have preferred to use those barbarous and meaningless names, Utopia, Anyder, Amaurote and Ademus. But, Gilles, since I see some people are so wary, that they can hardly be induced to believe what we simple and credulous folk have written down on the relation of Hythlodaye, lest my credit be in danger with them as well as the faithfulness of history, I am glad I may say on behalf of my offspring, what in Terence Mysis says about Glycerium's boy, lest he should be regarded as a changeling: 'I thank the gods that some free women were present when I was brought to bed.' For this also has fallen out very conveniently, that Raphael told his tale not merely to you but to many other respectable and worthy men, perhaps still more lengthily and weightily, certainly no less so, than he did to ourselves. But if these unbelievers will not believe them either, let them go to Hythlodaye himself; for he is not yet dead. I heard lately from some who came from Portugal, that on March 1st last he was as hale and sprightly as ever. So let them inquire the truth of him or, if they like, try him with questions, only I would have them understand that I am only responsible for my part and not for the credit of another. Farewell, dear Peter, and greet for me your charming wife and pretty little daughter, to whom my wife wishes long life.

ERASMUS OF ROTTERDAM TO JOHN FROBEN, HIS DEAR GOSSIP, GREETINGS

I have always hitherto been exceedingly pleased with all my friend More's writings, but on account of our close friendship, I somewhat distrusted my own judgment. But now I see that all learned men unanimously subscribe to my opinion, and even more warmly admire the man's preeminent genius—not that they have more affection, but that they have greater discernment—I am quite inclined to approve of my verdict, and shall not hesitate in future to express my opinion. What would not such natural endowments have accomplished, if his talent had been trained in Italy, if it had been entirely devoted to literature, if it had ripened to a proper harvest and its own autumn? When a mere youth, he wrote sportive epigrams, most of them when he was but a lad. He has never left his native country, except once or twice when serving his King on an embassy in Flanders. Not only is he married, and has family cares to attend to, not only does he hold an important public office, and has much legal business, but he is distracted by so many and weighty affairs of State, that you wonder he finds time even to think of books.

So I send you his early essays and the *Utopia*, that, if you think well, they may go out to the world and to posterity with the recommendation of being printed by you. For such is the reputation of your press, that if it is known that a book has come from the house of Froben, that is enough to recommend it to the learned world. Farewell, and greet for me your excellent father-in-law, your agreeable wife, and delightful children. My little godson, Erasmus, in whom I am as much interested as you, has been born in an atmosphere of scholarship: so mind that he is trained from the earliest years in all good learning.

LOUVAIN. 25th August 1517.

Printed in the United States
by Baker & Taylor Publisher Services